MUSTARD SEEDS

"This brave and lovely book will raise many downhearted spirits. Sensitive and thoughtful, it is filled with new beginnings, hope, and the wonder and beauty of the search for God."

— *Amy Blackmarr, Author*
Going to Ground: Simple Life on a Georgia Pond

"Reading *Mustard Seeds* feels like time spent conversing with a dear old friend over a cup of coffee. Lynn's honest story of how she renewed her faith in Jesus will be a blessing and a source of encouragement to her many new 'friends' who'll read this book."

— *Mickey McLean, Web Managing Editor*
WORLD Magazine

MUSTARD SEEDS

THOUGHTS ON THE NATURE OF GOD AND FAITH

LYNN COULTER

B&H
PUBLISHING GROUP
Nashville, Tennessee

Published by B&H Publishing Group,
Nashville, Tennessee

Dewey Decimal Classification: 248.84
Subject Heading: FAITH \ CHRISTIAN LIFE

1 2 3 4 5 6 7 8 9 10 11 12 13 14 15   12 11 10 09 08

To Bill and Michael,
with abiding love

In memory of
James and Juanita Baxter

Contents

Acknowledgments

Mary Wyman, thank you for your insightful reading, your prayers, and your dear friendship.

Roseanne Key, you've blessed us more than you will ever know. Jesus shines through your life.

John Tittle, former associate pastor at First Presbyterian Church of Douglasville, Georgia, thanks for sharing Bible verses and books with me and for the coffee and blessings that poured out from The Well.

Sandy Fox, associate pastor emeritus at First Presbyterian Church of Douglasville, Georgia, I'm grateful for your compassionate walk of faith with my family.

Thomas Walters, sincere thanks to you and all the good people of B&H Publishing for your hard work and dedication to this project.

Bill, thank you for your willingness to share our story.

Introduction

*Let us look only to Jesus, the One who began our faith
and who makes it perfect.*
—HEBREWS 12:2 NCV

Have you ever lost anything valuable—maybe a set of car keys, a special phone number, even your driver's license? Except for my glasses, which I misplace at least once a day (I've even found them, inexplicably, on top of the refrigerator), I'm pretty good at keeping up with things. That's probably why I remember the first time I lost something that really mattered.

I was about ten years old, a kid growing up in a little Georgia town. Back then our church encouraged children to attend Sunday school each week by giving us lapel pins, ribbons, and other trinkets for perfect attendance. I was big on collecting things, so I'd already accumulated a fistful of awards when our teacher clapped her hands one morning and made an announcement. In an effort to avoid the usual drop in attendance that happened every summer when school let out, she was going to give away something extra special. Every child who came to class throughout the vacation season would get a charm—a little mustard seed encased in a clear plastic bubble. Each boy would get a key chain to clip onto his charm, while the girls could slide theirs onto necklaces. She let us pass around one of the slender chains while she started a lesson on faith.

Even with the slight magnification of the plastic bubble, the mustard seed looked tiny. When it was my turn to hold it, I marveled at its size while the teacher explained how even a little faith could move a mountain. All we needed, she said, was a drop of belief no bigger than the mustard seed and we could do anything through Christ, who made us strong.

I was listening, but the teacher's lesson wasn't sinking in. Faith was a concept I'd never thought about very much and didn't really understand. I'd heard people talk about having faith, of course, and the word popped up often enough in the hymns we sang or the Scriptures the pastor read aloud. I thought I probably had plenty of it, if faith meant religious belief, because I'd already accepted Jesus as my Savior and had been baptized.

Still, I was beginning to get the idea that this faith business was more than just acknowledging God as the Creator and Jesus as his Son. It also sounded as if faith were something deeper and more complex, like a kind of trust or confidence you were supposed to have in your heavenly Father even when really bad things happened. Looking back, I can see why the concept sounded vague and confusing to me. After all, I lived in a small, safe community with two loving parents. Soon I would have a new baby sister, and I had friends to play with, a clean school to attend, and nice teachers. I had everything a fourth grader needed, and I was too young and sheltered to realize how vast and complicated the world could be. So what did the Sunday-school leader mean about moving mountains, anyway, and why should I care about them? *Faith* was a word that fluttered right out of my head, and the only time I remembered it was when I thought about that mustard-seed necklace. I set my sights on earning one, and by the time the poplar trees and dogwoods were dropping gold- and ruby-colored leaves on the church lawn, my teacher was helping me fasten a shiny gold chain around my neck.

I don't remember taking my necklace off after that, and I'm pretty sure I wore it all through my fifth-grade year. But then something happened. Maybe I unhooked it one afternoon the next summer, right before I jumped into the clear blue water at the municipal swimming pool, or when the chain turned my skin a funny moss-green color because the necklace was only a cheap thing, after all, and certainly not real gold. Maybe the fragile links snapped, and the mustard seed in the clear bubble fell to the ground and rolled away out of sight. So many years have passed, I simply can't remember. I'm only aware that at one time I wore my necklace every day; but much later, when I wanted to put it on again, I couldn't find it.

My loss wasn't so bad, as losses go, not like dropping a wedding ring down the drain or having your wallet stolen. The little mustard-seed charms were probably mass-produced and bought in bulk for pennies. Still, I loved it, and I'd often turned the charm around and around in my fingers, puzzling over how something so small had come to stand for something as important and mysterious as faith.

Today I have a child of my own, a son who has never been particularly interested in Sunday-school giveaways and who doesn't wear any jewelry besides a watch and his high-school ring. I described the lost necklace to him once, and though he was sympathetic, he didn't understand why I'm still talking about it years later.

I could probably find another mustard-seed charm if I tried. Jesus' parable about faith is widely known, and I'm sure there are manufacturers who make the trinkets. But I miss my necklace because of the Sunday-school lesson about faith that came with it. I still think about that mustard seed because a few years ago I almost lost something far more valuable than any necklace. A few years ago, I almost lost my faith.

Seems I never had a strong hold on faith to begin with, despite all those mornings I showed up regularly for Sunday school and worship services. I just didn't realize how weak it was until my family faced a series of crises. As our trials dragged on for year after year, stress and grief consumed me and left me wondering where God was and whether he really cared for us.

I don't mean to suggest that what my family experienced was anything unusual or special; at some time in life everyone suffers when a loved one dies or when there's a traumatic injury or illness. Job loss and broken relationships are ordeals for anyone who experiences them. Being human means encountering pain.

Sometimes, however, suffering can go on for so long, or run so deep, that faith begins to falter. We can be desperate for God's presence, but in our confusion and fatigue, we don't know how to find him. We long to hear a word from him, but we're surrounded by chaos, and there's no quiet place to retreat and listen for his voice. That's when some of us wear out, give out, and give up. We decide, in our despair and anguish, that either God doesn't care or he isn't even there at all.

Sadly, that's what I decided.

I decided that God did not care for me, even though I had attended church for years and volunteered at Vacation Bible School. I started wondering whether he was real, despite the fact that I often read books about spirituality and religion and I had several Bible translations sitting on my bookshelves. I doubted him, even though I'd sung in the choir, taught children's classes, joined prayer groups and women's circles, and completed Bible-study courses. I'd done all the standard things we think characterize a life of faith and trust in God—but none of them made a difference when my life imploded because my faith, as it turned out, was green and untried, as weightless as air, as fleeting as a breath, as insubstantial as smoke.

When my mother died and my father became ill, when my husband lost his job, when I shattered my shoulder and couldn't work for months, I called out to God for help, and I thought I received nothing but silence. "Why?" I demanded of him, deeply hurt at first by my loss, but later, bitter and angry that God would take so much away. I couldn't see any hope. Sad and sick at heart, I finally turned my back, ready to walk away. I was finished, I told myself, with this false and misleading thing, this ridiculous hope, this lie called faith.

But here is the good news: God didn't let me go. He didn't let me walk away, just as he refuses to let any of his broken, lonely, sad, hurting children go when they honestly seek him. God sends Jesus, the Good Shepherd, to find his sheep and bring them home when they wander.

God called me back to faith in a hundred ordinary little ways: through a friend's loving words, an encouraging phone call, a timely note or card in the mail. He opened my eyes to see and appreciate his myriad daily gifts: the freshness in the air after rain blows through; a wren's nest built in an old motorcycle helmet atop a pile of trash; the sweet, gritty taste of pears; the deep shade in a grove of pecan trees; the cool, damp feel of morning fog; fat blackberries hanging from prickly vines; my son's laugh; dark nights that helped me sleep; the sound of a rooster's throaty wake-up call. God has given me a wake-up call through all these tender mercies and many more.

I'm not perfect. I still stumble and doubt and question, but I believe God is big enough to handle our questions, and I believe he understands and forgives our doubts and fears. He comforts us with the promise that no matter what, Jesus will wash away our sins and make our hearts as pure and clean as snow.

I went out looking for God, and thanks to his grace, I found him. Then again, it's probably more accurate to say that he found me.

The mustard-seed necklace is gone forever, I'm afraid, but faith turned out to be the real treasure I should have been guarding anyway. Now that I have faith back, I don't want to lose it again. I want to be steadfast, sure, and confident that God is always at hand, no matter what my circumstances, because the Bible says that his nature is to be faithful: "If we are faithless [do not believe and are untrue to Him], He remains true (faithful to His word and His righteous character), for He cannot deny Himself" (2 Tim. 2:13 AMP). Or, as the Message translation says so perfectly, "If we give up on him, he does not give up—for there's no way he can be false to himself."

When Peter, also called Simon, heard Jesus speak about his own death, and shortly before he denied Jesus three times in a single night, Jesus said, "Simon, Simon, look out! Satan has asked to sift you like wheat. But I have prayed for you that your faith may not fail. And you, when you have turned back, strengthen your brothers" (Luke 22:31–32 HCSB). It's comforting to know that God lets us turn back, because he's the God of second chances—or third or fourth chances, if that's what it takes. Now that I've turned around, I'd like to encourage my brothers and sisters in Christ by saying, hold on. God is real. He cares. Believe in him—and believe him.

The Scriptures tell us that a tiny mustard seed can grow into a plant strong and sturdy enough to shelter God's weakest creatures. My prayer is that my faith, and yours, will grow strong enough to shelter our lives. As you read these pages, I hope you will find refreshment and encouragement for your spirit. May you always have the limitless hope, the lasting joy, and the perfect peace that comes from knowing God's deep and abiding love.

Chapter 1

Yearning for God

*If the only prayer you say in your life
is thank you, that would suffice.*
—MEISTER ECKHART

I was making my way through Atlanta's rush-hour traffic one afternoon, dodging orange construction barrels and other drivers zipping through the crowded lanes, when a road sign caught my eye. Rest Stop Ahead, it promised, pointing to one of those green oases positioned along the interstates, a spot with trees and picnic tables and a patch of grass where weary travelers can stretch their legs.

Any other time I might have pulled off to grab a cup of coffee until the traffic cleared out, but the sign meant something else to me that day, and I was eager to get to my destination. The "rest stop" I was headed toward was a weekend retreat at the Monastery of the Holy Spirit, a small community of Cistercian monks, better known as Trappists, about thirty-five miles east of Atlanta. I'd heard about the monastery for years, a place where several generations of monks lived together, worshipping under the soaring Gothic arches of an old abbey church and working to support their mission by selling homemade fudge and fruitcakes, bonsai trees, and little pots of fragrant herbs. I was longing to experience the peace and solitude the monastery was known for.

I hadn't known much peace for the past several years, not since my mother became ill in April 2001. Our relationship had always been warm and close. Even though we lived just twenty minutes apart, I liked to curl up in my old armchair and talk to her on the phone every night.

Mama had never been sick with anything more than a cold or the flu, so when she began having some unusual symptoms, I urged her to see her family physician. He immediately made an appointment for her with an oncologist, and a few days later my father and I accompanied her when she went to his office to get her test results.

The doctor's receptionist ushered us into a consultation suite that looked like someone's elegant living room. Glossy travel books covered a coffee table, and a little fountain with Japanese figurines bubbled in one corner. There were plush chairs, a sofa, and table lamps with soft, low lighting. This didn't look like any doctor's office I'd ever seen before, and my stomach lurched as I guessed that this lovely, relaxing room was designed for a special purpose. It was intended to be a comfortable and comforting place for patients who were about to hear terrible news.

And what we heard was terrible. The doctor spoke compassionately and encouragingly, but underneath his kind tone, the message was clear: my mother had a rare and aggressive form of lymphoma, and there was no cure. The only treatment was the standard chemotherapy for more common kinds of cancer, but he did not believe it would hold this disease at bay for very long. Most patients survived less than two years.

By Thanksgiving, seven months later, I was standing over an ironing board pressing one of my mother's favorite pink suits, the one we'd chosen to bury her in, while my nose ran and tears dripped down my face and onto the cloth. She was ten days away from her seventieth birthday, and her present—tickets my sister and I had bought to take her to a holiday play—were still in my purse.

Previously in May—one month after my mother's diagnosis—my husband, Bill, lost his job. After working for one employer for almost a decade, he'd resigned to accept what sounded like a better opportunity at a different firm. Little did we know that the national economy was already sinking into a recession fueled by widespread job outsourcing and the crash of the so-called dot-com stocks.

After the layoff, Bill, like many others in the country who'd lost jobs, sent out hundreds of résumés and cover letters. He networked with business acquaintances and friends. He worked by the hour when someone needed to install a new water heater or move furniture. A few interviews popped up, months apart, but there were no offers, not even for part-time positions.

It would take an entire year for another full-time job to surface. Even when the economy began showing signs of improvement, experts agreed that this was largely a "jobless recovery."[1]

Any job loss is traumatic because our sense of self is so intricately bound up with the work we do. Our family's situation took a devastating toll on us financially as well, since Bill received only one month of severance pay. The checks I was getting for my contract work didn't stretch very far, and when his state unemployment benefits ran out, we were forced to deplete our savings to avoid losing our home. As time passed and the job situation remained grim, we resorted to charging even our groceries on credit cards. Daily I ripped open our mail and felt queasy when I looked at our mounting debts. By juggling mailing dates and cutting expenses to the bone, we managed to scrape together each minimum payment and avoid defaulting on any of them. However, as the months rolled by, I wondered how much longer we could hold on. Bankruptcy was a possibility that trailed us like a shadow.

After twelve months of unemployment, the job market in the Southeast slowly began to open up again, and one morning a recruiter in South Carolina called Bill about an opportunity. He interviewed three times, and we were ecstatic when the employer made an offer. The position sounded great, but Bill nearly turned it down because the company wanted us to relocate. At seventy-five, my dad was too heartbroken and sick after my mother's death to move with our family, and leaving him behind was not an option. Eventually, Bill came up with an alternative: he took the out-of-state job and moved into a trailer park. Every Monday at 4:30 a.m., he got up and drove to his new office, worked all day, and went "home" to his trailer, which sat in the sun in a row of other little trailers in an unpaved lot on the outskirts of Greenville. On Fridays he worked eight hours, clocked out at 5:00 p.m. or later, and drove three hours back to Atlanta to spend the weekend with us. He did this for a year and a half, getting up early on winter mornings to scrape off the ice that formed on the inside of the trailer windows and sitting outside on summer evenings when the oppressive heat overwhelmed his small air-conditioning unit.

Meanwhile, I stayed in our home in Georgia so our son, Michael, could finish out the year at his middle school while my sister and I took turns caring for our dad, whose health and spirits continued to decline. Bill's last-resort arrangement saved our house, but living apart took every penny we could earn as we scraped to pay for two sets of utilities, as well as for gas, long-distance phone calls, and trailer-park fees. We were miserable. Please God, I pleaded. Help us.

Then one day my dad slipped and fell, breaking two verte-brae in his back that had been weakened by undiagnosed osteo-porosis. We asked God to relieve his constant pain, which stub-bornly refused to respond to the medicines and spinal blocks and surgery his doctors tried. When he sat at the dinner table, picking at his plate in silence, or lay in his darkened bedroom for hours watching TV, I also pleaded with God to ease his ter-rible grief. His heart was failing, the doctor said, but we knew that. His emotional heart had died with my mother, so it was no surprise to hear that his physical one was broken as well.

Please, I kept asking, please send Bill a job back home so we can be together again. Send me more work so we don't have this constant stress of trying to pay our bills. Please help Michael, who misses his father during the week and cries when he drives away to South Carolina every Monday before dawn.

Ask, and you will receive, the Bible says, but what I asked for and what I got were not the same things. While Bill was living out of state, I had an accident. I moved the dog's bowl one morning and spilled her water, but because I was in a hurry—I was always in a hurry back then, trying to cope with so many things at once—I didn't mop it up. It was a stupid, silly mistake, and I paid for it. Later, as I ran through the kitchen—hurrying again—I slipped in the water and fell against the sharp corner where two walls met. The hard, freak blow dislocated my shoulder and shattered the bones at the joint.

"How did this happen?" the puzzled doctor kept asking me in the emergency room. Since he couldn't put a cast around a shoulder joint, he strapped me into an elastic brace that immobilized my entire left side from my shoulder to my fingertips. The bones grew back imperfectly, but at least this treatment, along with six months of physical therapy, let me avoid joint-replacement surgery and gave me back most of the use of my arm.

In spring 2003, soon after I finished therapy, another recruiter called Bill, this time with a job offer much closer to our home, so he gladly accepted and closed up the trailer in Greenville. It didn't take long for trouble to find us again. The new company soon had a layoff, too, and after only five months, Bill was back at the unemployment office. It was three days before Christmas 2003.

In spring 2004, on the evening of Mother's Day, my father went to sleep and did not wake up again.

That summer, Bill found another job, this time with a stable company, and at last the layoff cycle was over.

In three years, both parents gone. Two layoffs, one lasting a full year. Three jobs. An eighteen-month separation while our family lived in different states. A serious injury and a painful recuperation. Staggering debts. And over all that happened to us personally, the national tragedy of 9/11.

During that time, I almost lost my faith. I prayed for God to help us so many times, and things only seemed to get worse. I inventoried my life over and over, wondering if God wasn't responding because, somehow, I was at fault, and I desperately tried to put right anything in me that seemed wrong. I waited and watched for his help to appear, but eventually my hope ran out.

Psychologists say that the most stressful events in our lives are the deaths of loved ones, job loss, injury, illness, financial problems, and separation. We'd had all of those in three years, and we knew it would take much longer to pay off our accumulated debts.

"Why, God?" I asked when these things happened. I swung from sorrow and grief to frustration and bewilderment and then to hot anger. I felt abandoned and forsaken. "You don't care," I told God from the bottom of my bitter heart. "You are not real. You are not there."

Throughout those wretched years, I tried to keep going. I did all the ordinary things ordinary people do every day. I worked, cleaned my house, and did the laundry. I helped my son with his homework and drove him to band practice. When my father died, I executed his estate, settled his complicated financial affairs, repaired and sold his house, and gave away my parents' last possessions.

And I became incredibly tired. One day, in the middle of all this trouble and grief, I drove to the grocery store to buy a pizza for dinner. I pushed a shopping cart into the frozen-foods section, reached for the freezer door, and felt myself hit an invisible wall. Suddenly I couldn't do one more thing. Not one. I couldn't open the freezer door. I couldn't figure out which brand of pizza to pick up. I just stood in the middle of the grocery store, hung my head, and cried.

Another shopper, a stranger, saw my distress and came over to put her arms around me. I couldn't get my breath long enough to explain. "Whatever it is," she whispered, "God will take care of you."

I tried to remember her words, but for a long time any peace I managed to find was a fragile thing, easily disrupted by the next problem or debt or illness. I yearned for God, but I was struggling to believe in him.

Time passed. God did not send me any miracles, at least not the kind we usually expect. My family didn't experience any earthly healings or reap any financial windfall. Our car's transmission went out. The health insurance we paid for through Bill's new employer became so expensive we had to scrimp even more to hang on to it. Our lives stayed messy and sad for a long time, and most days we simply slogged along as best we could. We got up each morning and went to work. We came home and slept. We got up and did it all over again the next day.

But as the months went by, my feelings of abandonment and anger toward God began to change. My grief for my parents was as deep as ever, but time does lessen some things, and my sense of loss became less raw, less of an open wound. Around the time my mother died, a woman I'd never met struck up an e-mail correspondence with me. This woman had experienced many of the same problems we were having, yet she had continued to walk with Jesus. Through this stranger's compassion and love and encouragement, I started to open my mind once more to the possibility that God could and did love me and my family, in spite of all that had happened. In my heart of hearts, I wanted very much to believe in God. I longed for a divine love that would never let me go. I yearned to believe everything that happened had some sort of meaning or purpose. What would it say about God, I wondered, if this kind of pain turned out to be pointless and wasted, just something to endure and not of any help to anyone?

As my new e-mail friend stayed in touch, gently ministering to me about God's goodness and trustworthiness, the tough shell around my heart began to split. One day I heard

a song written by Leonard Cohen called "Anthem," and I recognized myself in its lines. Cohen had written that it was OK
to be broken because light can stream through our damaged
places. My heart and spirit had been broken; but as it turned
out, the warm light of God's love was going to shine through
those cracks, just as Cohen had said.

I began reading some excellent books about spirituality and
Christianity by authors such as Beth Moore, Philip Yancey,
Max Lucado, and C. S. Lewis, searching for reasons to help
me understand why God allows pain and suffering. All right, I
mentally challenged each author as I flipped through his or her
pages: *Explain all this to me—go ahead. Why do my prayers seem to
go unheard? Is God holding himself apart from me? Have we done
anything to deserve what has happened in our lives?* The books
were filled with good information and intriguing clues about
God's nature and purposes, but I also decided to go back to the
source. I started reading the Bible again, and this time I read it
in an altogether new and different way. I began to identify with
many of the characters I found in its pages, especially the ones
who were imperfect and weak, or who also peppered their con-
versations with God with the word *why*. Suddenly Jesus' words
sounded as if they'd been meant especially for me.

Little by little, I started to see and count up the blessings God
had given me, and to trust in his love, even though I accepted
that I might never understand everything that had happened to
us. I thanked him for giving me friends and for the blessings of
my loving husband and son. I cultivated gratitude for the new

jobs that were providing for our needs. I was alive, and I learned to count life itself as a marvelous gift. Finally, I praised him for the promise of eternal life and the hope of seeing my parents again in heaven.

One day, an editor I knew mentioned that her magazine was looking for an essay about a spiritual journey. I asked her to send me on a retreat to the Trappist monastery so I could write about my experiences, and she agreed.

Some of my friends wondered what I was doing and predicted that I wouldn't be able to make it through the three-day retreat without my e-mail or computer. The world runs too hard and fast, they told me, and you won't be able to slow down that much, even for a long weekend.

It was hard to explain, but I really felt a desire to go. I was looking for some deep healing and for some comfort from a God who had seemed distant for too long. From what I had read, a silent retreat also would follow the example of some of the Bible's greatest spiritual seekers. In the Old Testament, Samuel became quiet so he could hear God. Elijah climbed a mountain to listen for God's gentle whisper. Habakkuk stood guard at his lonely post to wait for the Lord's instructions. The Scriptures tell us that after his conversion the apostle Paul went alone into Arabia. And of course, the Bible reminds us that Jesus often stepped away from crowds of followers to spend time alone with his heavenly Father.

As a Protestant, I'd hesitated to visit the monastery, although I knew it must have been established in great faith when it was built in 1944, when Catholics made up a scant 4 percent of Georgia's population. I was welcomed warmly as I checked in and was directed to a tiny room with a shared bath. A sign in the lobby politely reminded me that complete silence was observed beyond the front desk. We retreatants were asked not to speak in the dining area, the halls, or the dormitory-style rooms.

There were few distractions there, even for my noisy mind. The simple room I was given held a nightstand with a lamp, a desk and chair, a Bible and a few books, and a single bed. I was invited to borrow from a small bookcase down the hall, but instead, I chose to flip through a journal of comments left by previous retreatants. One visitor had written a striking description of a spiritual retreat as a kind of military strategy. It offered, he said, a chance to withdraw from battle and sufficient time to regroup oneself for victory.

The book was filled with praise for solitary retreats like the one I'd undertaken, but as the hours ticked by, I began to worry that the experience might not help me. I read and prayed, but the quiet started to weigh on me. My little room, with its oatmeal-colored walls and musty odor, felt claustrophobic. Being alone felt strange—and well, lonely—and even when I opened my door to the hallway or ventured out on the grounds, I seldom saw any of the other half-dozen retreatants who had also come for the weekend.

Soon after I arrived, a thunderstorm erupted. Wind pushed the rain through open doorways and under awnings, so for the rest of the day, I dodged cloudbursts to dash between the monastery gardens and the shadowy church. Determined to play fair, I resisted calling home, and when the sun popped out, I strolled down to the lake. Bill and Michael knew where to find me if they needed me, and I wanted to focus on God.

At dinnertime I found a seat at a long table in the quiet dining room. Each retreatant left an empty chair on either side and sat facing forward in the same direction so no one looked directly at anyone else. It seemed very odd to eat this way. Conversation was permitted in another room down the hall, but no one used it.

I took a bowl of vegetable soup from the serving line and sat with my head bowed as I ate. It was warm and delicious, filled with fresh carrots, snap beans, and tender chunks of new potatoes, like the homemade soup my mother had made, and I wondered whether the vegetables had come from the monks' own garden.

Each day we retreatants were invited to worship with the monks for vigils at 4:00 a.m., Mass with lauds at 7:00 a.m., and vespers at 5:20 p.m. There were midmorning and mid-afternoon prayers and compline, or night prayers, at 7:30 p.m. I attended some of the services on the first day I arrived but felt confused. Nothing in my Presbyterian upbringing, or during the years we'd attended a Baptist church, had prepared me to understand the order of the hymns and psalms we were supposed to recite. I was frustrated by the antiphon, which proved to be a kind of call and response, and realized too late that I should have read up on the services before I'd come.

I slept uneasily that first night and woke up with a backache and a sense of disappointment. I was supposed to be thinking of spiritual things, not the thinness of the mattress on my cot, and I even found myself distracted by a column of ants that showed up to march across my nightstand.

But things began to change during the second day of the retreat. Instead of feeling odd, the silence and the solitude started to soothe me. When I picked up my Bible and walked down to the monastery's lake to read, the chaotic noise that always played in my head, the worries and doubts and questions, finally stopped. I was able to rest and pray while I watched a flock of geese dabble in the water.

In the afternoon I slipped into a classroom to join a talk given by the monks, who reminded me of wise, old teachers in their simple robes and leather sandals. On the last day of my retreat, one monk mentioned tending a garden, which explained the dirt on the jeans he wore under his black robe. I found myself wondering whether he'd just come in from weeding his vegetables, like the ones we'd had in our soup the previous night. *Digging,* I thought, *is hard work.*

"Dig," he said suddenly, and the hairs on my neck prickled to hear him echo my thoughts. "Read the Scriptures, and be patient. Let the Word soak into your life."

His words resonated with me because I'm a gardener, too, and the truth in his short lecture jumped out. I needed to persevere and keep digging. I needed to read my Bible not just when I was discouraged or sad but every day. I needed to continue my prayers of thanksgiving and praise, not just grumble about my problems and wants.

In *Believing God*, author Beth Moore describes how it's sometimes necessary to fight for faith, the way soldiers grapple on a battlefield, trusting God for the victory when it takes all we've got to get through a single day.[2] I've found this to be true. We may be called to walk through difficult seasons that feel as if they'll never end. We can nearly succumb to exhaustion or depression. Other people may turn out to be the source of our problems, or we may find that we've brought them on ourselves through our own poor decisions and wrong choices. In the end, the only thing that really matters is that we plant our feet firmly on the ground of faith. Don't be afraid, the Bible says, but hold fast and "see the LORD's salvation He will provide for you. . . . The LORD will fight for you" (Exod. 14:13–14 HCSB). When God does the fighting, he will take the field and win the day.

My journey back to a sustaining and enduring faith has been long and slow, but I've found help along the way. I've met people who stood patiently with me, without judging, while I raged and suffered and questioned. Sandy, our now-retired associate pastor, met with me for counseling. A Stephen's Minister named Max served as a godly resource and prayer partner for Bill. A friend, Jane, checked her son out of school on the day of my mother's funeral so that Michael would have someone his age to talk to, a gesture of friendship and compassion that touched me deeply.

No, God didn't show himself to me in the "big things." There was no miracle cure, no check in the mail, no voice from the mountaintop. Instead, I learned to look for signs of him in the small blessings of daily life. I saw his hand in the goldfinches that feasted on the seeds in my dying garden each fall and in the music the frogs made on rainy nights. I felt him in the way my old dog used to nuzzle me with her rough nose and in the times my husband let me soak his shirt with tears. I found his compassion in the teenage friend who made us a sympathy card with paper and colored pencils and in the neighbors and church members who called to check on us and say they cared.

I reread my Bible and learned to really love the humble, gentle Jesus who healed a blind man with mud and spit. I longed for the fellowship he showed to his disciples when he ate a meal of bread and fish with them after his resurrection, a gesture that helped put their doubts to rest.

Life is filled with mystery, and it always will be, and I had to learn to trust him, to take the bitter with the sweet and believe that both came from his hand. My writing buddy Jim once told me that God isn't supposed to make life easy, but I've found that he can and does make life good.

I am just an ordinary woman, a wife, a mother, and a writer. I am not a scholar or a theologian. I am just another person who has suffered loss and who needs God every single moment of every single day. Because of that, I choose to walk in faith.

The Bible promises that when you look for God and you give your search everything you've got—"all your heart [and mind] and soul and life"—you'll find him (Deut. 4:29 AMP). We're not guaranteed the resolution to every earthly problem, but I can live in the tension because I'm persuaded of one perfect, powerful, unwavering thing: God loves us. He gave his only Son to make sure we know it, and he promises eternal life to those who accept and believe in him.

We have God's own Word to testify to who he is and what he's all about. When I read the Scriptures, I imagine them as his love letters to a hurting world, and that helps restore my spirit.

Before I left the monastery that weekend, I found a quote by Thomas Merton, a respected Trappist monk and author, posted in a hallway, and I stopped to copy it down. Merton admitted that he, too, sometimes had difficulty following the road he was given to walk, but he said he always desired to know and do the Father's will.

If we get lost and confused in our own lives, we don't have to worry too much about which road to follow, as long as we are following Jesus. "I am the way, the truth, and the life," he said in John 14:6 (HCSB), and Paul, writing to the church at Ephesus, added, "It's in Christ that we find out who we are and what we are living for. Long before we first heard of Christ and got our hopes up, he had his eye on us, had designs on us for glorious living, part of the overall purpose he is working out in everything and everyone" (Eph. 1:11–12 MSG).

We won't always understand why certain things happen, but we can live with not knowing, confident that God is in control. As Paul urged the Philippians, we can "be glad in God!" (Phil. 3:1 MSG) because "God, who makes everything work together, will work you into his most excellent harmonies" (Phil. 4:8–9 MSG).

Every quest for faith begins with a yearning for God. I want to be in the center of his will and a part of his excellent harmonies, so now, when I'm outdoors tending my garden, I try to remember the lessons I've learned. When I'm on my knees, pulling weeds or planting, I remember to stop from time to time to simply bow my head and say, "Thank you."

Seeds of Faith

God, you never let go of me! I'm so grateful for the glorious love you showed the world through Jesus, your Son. Let your Word grow in my life and illuminate my darkness. Amen.

Therefore as you have received Christ Jesus the Lord, walk in Him, rooted and built up in Him and established in the faith, just as you were taught, and overflowing with thankfulness.

Colossians 2:6–7 HCSB

Chapter 2

Used People

Help, GOD—the bottom has fallen out of my life!
—PSALM 130:1–2 MSG

I know a thing or two about used cars. My dad bought me the only new vehicle I've ever owned, an olive-green coupe with a fake alligator-hide roof. It sounds horrible now, but at age eighteen, I thought it looked pretty hot. "Hot" didn't describe the puny engine, though, which practically chugged going uphill. Even though I was a careful and conscientious driver, the little engine gave out before it hit forty thousand miles.

Since then, I've been paying for my own wheels, and it's been lemons all the way. We once bought a thirdhand luxury car, marveling that we'd found a nice sedan at a bargain-basement price. Too bad we weren't tipped off by the Florida owner's eagerness. There was a world of rust hiding on that car's salt- and sand-weathered undercarriage.

Our next disaster was an old station wagon. Between its black body paint and big windows, the interior heated up like a greenhouse every time we drove it, making it more suitable for raising hothouse orchids than dashing to the store for spaghetti sauce.

In hindsight, it's easy to joke about used cars, but it's not funny at all when you're depending on some old heap to get to work or take your kids to school. Cars don't last forever, no matter how carefully you maintain them. By the time we bought ours, most of them were already shot. I didn't know much about used cars when I started out, but I've learned plenty since then.

I also know a few things about used people, having been one myself.

Used people are the ones who feel ready for the scrap heap of life. They're people who have been worn out by jobs that drive them too hard or spouses who abuse them. Some lives stall out when unemployment hits, or loneliness. Others are wrecked by spending too much time in a divorce lawyer's office or a jail cell. Needy friends who suck up precious time and energy can take a toll. Addictions and jealousy, anxieties and anger do their share of body damage.

If you've struggled with chronic insomnia or wondered whether anyone will ever love you, if you've been forced to surrender a lifelong dream or found yourself in a dead-end job, if you've been lied to or cheated on, if you've found yourself living with a teenager you can't trust or a parent who criticizes everything you do—you may wind up on the long list of used people too.

When troubles multiply, life can hit the skids, and even the stoutest hearts wind up battered and bruised. More than one strong spirit has bowed to too much stress or a wicked-busy schedule.

Fil Anderson knows what it's like to wear out. He was a freshman in college when he jumped at the chance to serve as a part-time youth pastor for his home church. Fil was just eighteen then, an age when many kids are still waiting tables or ringing up cash registers; but he was already crazy in love with God, and he plunged happily into his new work. Before long, he was delighting in his grateful congregation's praises, and deservedly so.

But he was working hard, and even young guys can get tired. By the time he was twenty, Fil was starting to feel weary. He was also beginning to question whether he was really equipped to handle the many responsibilities that came with his position, but his schedule was too packed to stop long enough to sit down and think about it. Anyway, he felt good about making a difference, and soon his work was attracting attention. Before long, he was asked to move to another church with a fast-growing membership, where he became a full-time pastor.

With more on his plate than ever before, Fil felt a sort of desperation settling in. "I was in over my head," he admits in his book, *Running on Empty: Contemplative Spirituality for Overachievers*, "but I would rather die than admit that, so I learned a simple lesson that seemed to provide the direction I needed: Just stay busy."[1] Unfortunately, busyness came with a high price. By the time he blew out twenty-one candles on his birthday cake, Fil was coming undone.

That winter, the young minister developed a teeth-chattering, chest-aching case of pneumonia. Worried about what his congregation would think if their hardworking leader took to bed, Fil slowed down for only five days before hurrying back to his office. A relapse quickly followed, and this time Fil climbed back into bed with severe double pneumonia. As depression and fatigue set in, he realized that the germs that knocked him off his feet weren't the real problem. Something else was going on, and no antibiotics were going to cure that disease.

"My lifestyle was making me sick," Fil confessed, "but I kept up the same insane pace."[2] Sometimes he found himself weeping and unable to stop, which frightened his parents and his mentor. At last he had to drop the mask he'd been living behind and ask for help. The following spring, Fil checked himself into a hospital psychiatric ward for some much-needed rest and healing.

For a while things got better. A compassionate doctor, a man of faith, helped Fil understand that God loved him unconditionally and wasn't keeping score of his accomplishments. But after Fil returned to his ministry, he picked up the pace, and again he felt himself sinking. Over and over, the destructive pattern repeated. Work. Get sick. Rest. Work again. Get sick again.

Then one day, Fil writes, he met Brennan Manning, a Christian author whose work he admired, and their fifteen-minute conversation helped Fil turn his life around. Manning listened as Fil confessed how hectic his life had become yet how spiritually empty he felt. You've got to slow down, Manning urged him. You're losing touch with the very same Jesus you're telling everyone else about.

By then Fil's faith was in crisis, and he had to work at not working. Gradually he learned to slow down and make room in his schedule for uninterrupted prayer and meditation. He devoted himself to spending more time with God instead of simply preaching about God and worked on building a closer relationship with his heavenly Father in the same way you'd build a relationship with anyone you love: by talking and listening.

The end result? "A profound sense of coming home to myself," Fil says.[3] Today he helps other people find their way home, too, through his work with Journey Resources, a spiritual guidance ministry based in Greensboro, North Carolina. The used-up man has become a man God uses in powerful ways.

Quirky California-based author Anne Lamott is no stranger to life's rock-bottom either. Alcoholic, sick, and drug-addled, she has written about hiking into town one day to buy a fresh bottle of whiskey when she passed an Episcopal church. Later, holed up in a dark room with the bottle she was slowly draining, Lamott faced a harsh truth. She realized that she could die if she continued on her self-destructive path and that her time might already be running out. When she remembered the church she'd passed earlier that day, she summoned up the guts to phone the rector and talk to him. It's been more than twenty years since Lamott made that call and found not only sanity and sobriety but also a lifesaving, soul-changing grace.[4]

Today Anne Lamott's readers savor her books about faith and redemption with their message of becoming refreshed, refilled, and downright juicy with life again. Her inspirational titles have become best sellers that point the way back to a God who knows a million perfect ways to turn used people around and to use those people to accomplish good things.

Of course, God isn't doing anything new when he picks us up, dusts off our sins and troubles, and sets us loose in the world again. He has always been able to turn brokenness into blessing. In the Old Testament, seventeen-year-old Joseph suffered terrible abuse at the hands of his jealous brothers, who threw him into a pit and sold him into slavery. Samson was betrayed by the woman he loved and trusted and found himself imprisoned by his enemies. Rahab let her body be used in prostitution; David cheated with another man's wife and sent him to his death. Jacob went lame after he wrestled through the night with a man who may have been an angel or God himself. Righteous Job, through no fault of his own, lost his children, his livelihood, and his health.

The characters in the New Testament didn't fare much better. Poor Mary Magdalene was possessed and tormented by evil spirits. Martha, as stressed and busy as any modern working mom, felt unappreciated and taken for granted, left alone to handle all the housework and cooking when guests came to visit. Jesus himself was hated, lied about, betrayed, beaten, and crucified. Yet God had a plan for each life.

The boy Joseph grew up to wear Pharaoh's ring as a sign of power and favor and opened the grain storehouses to save Egypt and his own family from starvation. Bound in bronze chains, blind Samson lifted his voice to God and was given the strength to bring down a host of Philistines. Rahab the harlot was blessed with the wits and courage to help two of Joshua's scouts escape from Jericho with their lives.

God changed lame Jacob's name to Israel and made him the father of nations. Job was restored, Mary was cleansed, and Martha learned—and now teaches us—a lesson about putting God first. In laying down his life, Jesus saved ours. Over and over, God has worked through the handicapped, the oppressed, the lonely, the poor, the sick, and the unappreciated to bless them and accomplish his purposes, and he will do the same for us today.

Who hasn't been misused by someone they loved and trusted, like Joseph?

Who hasn't felt stressed, like Martha?

Who hasn't come to the end of the rope, like Anne Lamott?

Who hasn't been exhausted, like Fil?

If I could have traded in my own used life a few years ago, I would have; but when I felt like giving up, God never gave up on me. The key word for used people is *anyway*. No matter what our circumstances are, God loves us anyway. No matter how bad things are, God is with us anyway. His love is enough to live on because it brings with it grace for today and hope for the future.

We "used people" don't always understand the reason for suffering and trials. Faith takes a beating when life treats us badly. We start to wonder where God is and what he's up to. Troubles mount up, and hope runs out. If there are lessons to be learned, well, we'd rather learn them some easier way, thank you very much.

Used people ask why a lot, at least until we figure out that why isn't the right question. We might find our answers down the road, or then again, we may not. Life isn't a paperback mystery, and we can't flip over to the last page to see how neatly the plot ties together. But there is an Author behind the scenes, and he knows exactly where each and every story is headed.

"Why" doesn't matter once you realize that God will never leave us, any more than he left Joseph in that pit or Job in his pile of ashes, Rahab in her shame or Martha in her indignant anger.

He knows how to transform what's wrong into what's right, and so ex-addict Anne Lamott is inspired to write books that sing of God's grace, former workaholic Fil Anderson is led to counsel people on their calling, and even I have learned to stop grumbling "Why?" and start asking, "What do I do with the life you've given me? How can I live in ways that are pleasing to you?"

The One who made us knows how to restore us. He is the God of second chances and the God of infinite mercy.

Before Jesus was born, the prophet Isaiah told the world he was coming and encouraged us to hold on because, he said, "A bruised reed He will not break" (Isa. 42:3 NASB). If you've ever visited a garden after a storm, you know what he was talking about. When tall, slender grasses are pummeled by hail or heavy rain, their stems bend over and snap. Delicate flowers get beaten to a pulp. We can be pummeled, too, by the storms of our circumstances and situations, but the gardener of our lives won't let us be destroyed.

"Come to Me, all of you who are weary and burdened," Jesus said, "and I will give you rest" (Matt. 11:28 HCSB). When we've done too much, gone too far, or worked too hard, Jesus steps in to carry us. We may feel ourselves falling, but when we fall toward Jesus, he rescues us.

The Bible doesn't say that our lives will be easy, and that's one reason it is so believable. If Jesus had said, "Follow me, and the road will always be straight and smooth," we might think the Son of God was just another charlatan. After all, we know what we're up against. We've read the newspaper stories about terrorist plots and global pollution. We know every society is threatened by AIDS and cancer and heart disease. We realize that many children go to bed hungry at night, and some senior citizens are forgotten or mistreated. As much as we want to, we couldn't and wouldn't believe someone who promised us a perfect life on earth.

In fact, Jesus warned us to expect the very opposite: "You will have suffering in this world," he said. Nevertheless, he added, "Be courageous! I have conquered the world" (John 16:33 HCSB). The glorious good news of the gospel is that with Jesus we have hope. We weren't made for this world, and we have a better one waiting for us; but until we get there, we have a Savior and a loving Shepherd to stand beside us, comfort us, love us, and uphold us. We just need to keep looking at him instead of the things that are falling into ruin around us.

Given enough time, everything will show signs of wear and tear. Computer monitors will pop and fade to black one day, and the elbows of a favorite jacket will fray and rip. We'll have another birthday and hear our knees creak when we climb the bedroom stairs. We can buy another jacket or rub some cream on those aging knees, but we can't turn back the clock and make everything fresh and new again.

But Jesus can. God can. The One who colors a parrot's wings bright blue and sprinkles frost on our windshields, the Creator who makes the fireflies glow and the winds whistle as they carve the canyons is the One who gives us hope and a future.

"My purpose is to give them a rich and satisfying life," Jesus told his followers (John 10:10 NLT). He knows how we feel because he's been where we've been. And whatever we run out of—energy, help, joy, peace, or purpose—he is able to give back to us when we ask.

The Message translation of the Twenty-third Psalm says it all: "God, my shepherd! I don't need a thing. You have bedded me down in lush meadows, you find me quiet pools to drink from. True to your word, you let me catch my breath and send me in the right direction" (Ps. 23:1–3 MSG).

When a used car has gone as far as it can, it's time to trade it in for a newer model. When we've gone as far as we can go, it's time to trade in the lives we're living. We can put away whatever is old and worn and used up and let the One who made us in the first place handle the restoration work. He knows how to repair our faith until it's strong and solid. "Behold," he says, "I make all things new" (Rev. 21:5 KJV).

Seeds of Faith

O Lord, thank you for giving us second chances and new beginnings. Thank you for the fresh hope that springs up in us when we invite your precious Son to make his home in our hearts. Amen.

Return to your rest, my soul,
for the LORD has been good to you.
For You, [LORD,] rescued me from death,
my eyes from tears,
my feet from stumbling.
I will walk before the LORD
in the land of the living.
Psalm 116:7–9 HCSB

Chapter 3

Forced to the Ground

*Cast your cares on the L*ORD
and he will sustain you;
he will never let the righteous fall.
—PSALM 55:22 NIV

Here in the South tornadoes are as common in the fall as Friday-night football games. When masses of warm and cold air collide to generate these violent storms, forecasters break into our favorite TV programs with warnings that send us flying down the basement steps, flashlights and portable radios in hand, until the danger has passed. Except the danger didn't pass us by one unseasonably warm September night in 1995, when a weather phenomenon known as La Niña brewed up a lot of trouble in the Atlantic Ocean.

Bill was out of town on business that week, so it fell to me to read a bedtime story and tuck Michael, who was then just six years old, under his Mickey Mouse quilt. When he was settled, I snapped off the lights, closed his door, and stood in the hallway for a moment. When I'd let the dog out after dinner,

I'd noticed that the sky had turned purplish-gray, the color of an ugly bruise, and the air felt muggy and still. I found myself listening for the crickets that clicked and sang in our backyard, but everything seemed unnaturally quiet. The only sound I heard was the tick of the old clock on the fireplace mantle.

Earlier in the day we'd heard that Hurricane Opal was lashing the Florida panhandle with winds gusting up to 140 miles per hour. TV reporters in rain slickers had clutched their microphones and braced against the wind as they described waterfront homes being washed away, roofs blown off churches and schools, and boats ripped from their moorings and scattered around local marinas like bathtub toys. The storm had made landfall at Pensacola, where it devastated the city, and now Opal had begun screaming northward. As her winds lost speed, she had been downgraded to a tropical storm, but she was still spawning tornadoes as she headed our way. The weather service expected the bad weather to sweep through the Southeast and into the mid-Atlantic states during the night.

The strange silence didn't last. By the time I walked through the house to lock the front door, rain was pounding against the roof. It was nearly too hot and oppressive to sleep, but I got into bed and tried to settle down with a book and my prayers. The forecast was ominous, and I was alone with a first grader and a nervous golden retriever, but eventually I fell asleep.

Oddly enough, I awoke when the lamp on my nightstand flickered off. There was something heavy holding me down, and I had to reach to the foot of the bed to push away one hundred pounds of trembling dog before I could struggle to my feet. The house was bat-black, and in my sleepy confusion, I couldn't figure out why I couldn't turn the lamp back on. Then I peered outside and realized that the neighborhood was dark and all the streetlights were off. Thunder boomed in the distance. *That explains it,* I thought. Lightning had hit a transformer, knocking out the power. I opened the front door to find water flowing in sheets from our leaf-packed gutters.

The rain was hammering down. I groped my way to a battery-operated radio we kept in a closet and twirled the dial. An announcer was warning listeners to take cover immediately because the National Weather Service had been clocking wind gusts at seventy miles an hour. He mentioned a tornado in a county just south of us. Opal's fury would lash us within minutes.

I stumbled my way to Michael's room, tripping over the dog as she tried to weave between my feet, and roused him. Already the wind was shrieking through our half-open windows.

"That sounds like ghosts, Mama!" Michael cried as he scrambled out of bed. The eerie, moaning sound raised the hairs on my arms, too, but we didn't stop. Down the hall the tornado alarm on the radio was screeching, and we bolted for the basement.

We'd been in our house for only three months, after nearly a year of searching for a neighborhood with lots of kids and shady trees. We'd bought the property because we loved the acres of hardwoods that surrounded it and the little creek that ran at the bottom of our hill. As Michael and I raced downstairs to huddle on an old couch we'd left there when we moved in, I thought about all those hardwoods with a sinking stomach. It was autumn, and the trees were old and very tall. Many stood close to the house. I started praying that the wind wouldn't send them crashing down on our heads.

For what seemed like forever, the storm roared around us. When the panicked dog crawled onto the couch with us, we hugged her as the roof groaned and the trees cracked and popped in the wind. An aluminum trash can blew off our deck and clattered by, making us jump. Nuts and acorns, ripped from nearby branches, battered the metal basement door. I heard crashes and thuds and guessed what was happening outside: the oaks and hickories had held on to their leaves during the unusually warm fall, and now their leafy limbs were filling like sails in the wind. We'd already had several consecutive days of steady rain, and the ground was saturated, leaving the soil too wet and soft to hold on to the big trees. The wind was pushing the hardwoods over, ripping them out by their roots.

"Please God, keep us safe," I prayed.

At last the night grew quiet again. The wind stopped roaring; the rain slowed to a trickle and drip. The power stayed off, though, and remained out for several more days. We lay there in the inky-black darkness, unable to see a single star poking through the cloudy night sky.

Michael fell asleep then, and so did the dog. With both of them snoring, I closed my eyes and drifted off, too, and we stayed in our tangle on the sagging couch until daylight—big retriever, little boy, and me. Before I slept, I mumbled words of thanks that the house hadn't gone spinning off into the sky, like Dorothy's farmhouse flying off to Oz.

It's hard to imagine how peaceful a day can be after a terrible night, but the next morning dawned quiet and calm. I opened the front door to the strong smell of turpentine—it was the sap from dozens of splintered pine trees—and gasped. Our heavily wooded yard, with all the wonderful old shade trees, looked as if it had been bulldozed.

Just as I'd feared, the big hardwoods were broken and tossed like giant pickup sticks. One tree blocked our driveway. Another had fallen so close to the kitchen window, it left a trail of wet leaves plastered to the glass. Our neighbors' yards were also flattened. If you've ever flown into Atlanta's airport and admired the sea of green below, you know the city is famous for its trees. More than four thousand of those beautiful trees fell that night in Opal's storms. From Mexico and Central America all the way into Canada, the wind and rain carved a path of death and destruction.

Although we thanked God for our safety, we were saddened by the ruin we saw around us. More than twenty of our trees were down, and it took weeks to clean up the mess as we sawed their massive trunks into chunks, stacked brush and branches into piles, and burned debris. With every step we slipped on fallen acorns and pine cones until we raked them up by bucketloads and threw them into the woods, in hopes that some animals would find and eat them during the winter.

Grace kept us safe, but elsewhere things were far worse. In the morning's gray light, I wondered how long it would take for shattered lives and damaged property to be put right again.

It takes a tremendous force to knock a forty-foot tree to the ground after it has been growing for decades. There are tremendous forces that can knock your faith to the ground, too, no matter how long it has been growing.

Job knew what it was like to be slammed to the ground. The Bible tells us that he was a righteous man when Satan appeared and, with God's permission, began to test him. At first Job stood firm, even when his children perished and his livestock disappeared. He didn't flinch when he broke out in boils. He resisted when his own wife nagged him to curse God and die.

But soon a few friends came by to commiserate, and Job's faith in God's perfect authority began to wobble. He started to question what he could have done to deserve so much misery. His friends jumped on him. Well, they said arrogantly (having just left the embrace of their own safe families and the comfort of their nice homes), you must have brought this on yourself! Or surely your children sinned and put this punishment on your head. At any rate, it's a blessing to be corrected by God, so stop complaining.

Sadly, Job's friends didn't sound too different from a lot of well-meaning Christians who rush in to explain things when we're suffering. The Bible does give us some clues to God's purposes. As C. S. Lewis wrote, pain can be the megaphone God uses to grab our attention, and he can weld it to forge character or reveal his glory. But if *why* Job suffered was important, I think God would have told him; and if we need to know why we're going through trials, I believe he'll tell us that too. If he chooses not to reveal his purposes, we can tread lightly when we talk to others about what they're going through. We can't know what God has in mind for them, and we don't want to add to their problems by spouting clichés or self-righteous "answers."

God didn't want Job's friends diagnosing his case, either, and he told them to back off. What God had in mind, instead, was a lesson in trust.

When his troubles poured down like rain, Job forgot the years that God had blessed him. He forgot the good times with his sons and daughters and the devoted wife who stuck by him when life turned upside down. He overlooked the extended family of brothers and sisters who came every year to celebrate his children's birthdays. He had been the richest cattleman around, the owner of sheep, camels, oxen, and donkeys, and yet he shrugged off the decades God had provided him with plenty.

Job, in other words, was pretty much like the rest of us. When things were fine, he was God's man. When times got tough, his problems swamped him. "You throw me into the whirlwind and destroy me in the storm" (Job 30:22 NLT), he cried out in anguish. "Thrown face down in the muck, I'm a muddy mess, inside and out" (Job 30:16–19 MSG).

When life slings mud on the path, faith can slip and fall. A missionary goes overseas to carry the gospel, and we wonder why he winds up injured in a car accident and has to come home. Parents pray for their premature baby, but when she survives, they're stunned and heartbroken to learn she'll have a painful disability. Many of us get confused and upset because we're God's people and yet things don't turn out the way we expect. It's like picking up a bouquet of beautiful roses and getting stabbed by hidden thorns.

Faith can erode in a hundred insidious little ways. We can put off worshipping together because it's hard to get up early on Sunday morning. We might spend more time talking to a friend on a cell phone than talking to our truest Friend in prayer. We often set our hearts on a new car or pair of shoes and let our craving for material things separate our hearts from Jesus.

But there's no denying it's the disasters that usually leave us reeling. It's the big blows that rip faith into rags.

When Job lifted his face out of the mud long enough to shout, Hey, God, what are you doing to me? God replied, but he didn't explain. He responded to Job from a whirlwind, from the very center of a violent storm. Turns out he'd been there all along, close to Job even as he endured his agonizing and long ordeal.

I'm in charge here, God declared. I'm the one who tips over the rain barrels of heaven when the earth is dry. I make the sea creatures and the field mice. Nothing gets through to you without my permission or outside my authority. In other words, God is saying that he allowed Satan to try Job, and from this we can surmise that no trouble touches us, either, without God's consent. Kay Arthur, a Bible teacher and author, nails it in her book *As Silver Refined: Learning to Embrace Life's Disappointments*: whether we understand his ways or not, and whether we like them or not, God is sovereign.[1]

At last, Job got it. I'm convinced, he said humbly. I'm talking about things no human can fathom, while you, God, are limitless: "I admit I once lived by rumors of you; now have it all firsthand—from my own eyes and ears! . . . I'll never again live on crusts of hearsay, crumbs of rumor" (Job 42:1–6 MSG). Encountering the living God was enough to rekindle Job's faith and encourage his spirit, and it's enough for us too.

There's no storm so strong that God's love can't reach us through it. No night is so dark that Jesus can't find us.

Jesus himself "fell to the ground," Mark 14:35 (HCSB) tells us, when he prayed in the Garden of Gethsemane about his coming death. He knows how we feel when the worst happens because he's been there too. When we're forced to the ground, we can take comfort in knowing that he also spent time on his knees, sure that the Father was listening and confident that his plan would be right. "Fear not," the Bible says, and those two short words appear over and over again in Scripture, a welcome reassurance for those of us who are prone to panic or despair or surrender.

"I am with you always," Jesus promised (Matt. 28:20 HCSB). He's the one who accompanies us on that sudden trip to the emergency room and the one who goes with our loved ones when they put on a uniform and serve overseas. Jesus watches over the preschool playground and the college frat house. He cares about what happens around the office watercooler or in the kitchen. He frequents churches and drug-riddled neighborhoods and lives as close to the high-rises as he does to the homeless. When life flings us to the ground, he picks us up again.

When storms like Opal finally blow out, they leave a lot of debris behind, and there's a ton of cleanup work to do. Not every storm ends in a bright, peaceful morning. Clouds can hover overhead for a long time. Sometimes we're called to live out our entire lives with storm wreckage around us. Life can be hard. But God is faithful, and he does not forget us.

When you're slogging through the muck and you think you can't feel God's presence, don't trust your feelings. Feelings can shift like the direction of the wind, but God never does. He is "a refuge from the rain" (Isa. 25:4 HCSB).

It took about a year after Opal's tornado for us to finish cleaning up our yard. We paid a handyman to come out and grind down the huge stumps left by the fallen trees, and we trucked in loads of dirt to fill up the gouges left in the ground. We shoveled and raked and then scattered handfuls of grass seed everywhere. We bought little dogwoods and sugar maples and other saplings to replace the trees that were pushed over by the wind. We planted in hope and faith, believing that what we entrusted to the soil would thrive and that one day beauty would replace the ugliness around us. When the spring rains came, they were warm and soft and gentle, and we waited and watched until the earth turned green again and things began to grow.

Seeds of Faith

Lord, you won't let the storms overwhelm me. Help me see you in the whirlwind when it threatens to engulf me. Remind me that nothing touches me without your awareness and your permission. If I'm forced to the ground, lift me up. Give me patience as you work in my life to deliver me so I can give glory and honor to your name. Amen.

Alone with none but thee, my God,
I journey on my way.
What need I fear when thou art near
Oh king of night and day?
More safe am I within thy hand
Than if a host did round me stand.
                    Saint Columba (521–97)

Chapter 4

Be Still and Know

I am at rest in God alone;
my salvation comes from Him.
He alone is my rock and my salvation,
my stronghold; I will never be shaken.
—PSALM 62:1–2 HCSB

A couple of Christmases ago, Bill asked for an unusual gift. "I'd like a pair of headphones I've been reading about," he said, flipping through a catalog that had come in the morning mail. "Every time I have to fly to a job site, I wind up sitting near the engine or next to a crying baby, and by the time we land, I've got a headache." He pointed to one of the glossy pages. "How about these?"

I looked at the price and gulped. What, I asked, was so special about those headphones that made them worth the expense? Didn't the airline provide a pair he could use to watch a movie or listen to music? Sure, he said, but that wasn't the point. These headphones weren't made only to pick up sounds; they were also designed to block noise out.

At first I shook my head in amazement. Imagine, paying for silence! Then the longer I thought about the headphones, the more I understood their allure.

There just aren't many quiet places anymore. Hop onto an elevator and Muzak fills your ears. Standing in line at the bank or sitting at an airport gate? Look around and you'll see overhead monitors spouting the latest news and stock-market reports. Whether you're eating out or pushing a supermarket cart, music hums in the background. Dial a business number, and you can catch an entire concert while you hold for a service representative. Even at home, most of us turn on a TV or radio while we vacuum or type a report, as if we could actually hear their companionable chatter over our noisy work. The world really is too loud, I decided, and from then on I dropped my spare change into our piggy bank to save for those fancy Christmas earpieces.

Most importantly, we need some peace and quiet when we want to be with God. Henri Nouwen, the Catholic priest and author, argued that it is virtually impossible to develop a spiritual life if you never have any time alone. "Prayer," he added, "is first of all listening to God. It's openness. God is always speaking."[1]

Modern life has made us all into multitaskers who can stir the spaghetti while we juggle cell phones at our ears with toddlers bumping against our knees, but it's hard to hear what God is saying if we can't give him our undivided attention. I've never heard God's audible voice, so I have to get what he's telling me through circumstances, situations, and the way I interact with other people; but I can't do that when I'm distracted by dogs and doorbells, office chatter and conference calls.

When I was little, I thought prayer had only one direction: up. I prayed, and my words soared into heaven. But it turns out that prayer is a two-way street after all and not just a monologue like the ones on late-night television. It's supposed to be a conversation.

Unfortunately, even when I've managed to shut off all the noise in my house, I've discovered there's a lot of racket coming from inside my head too. Martin Hope Sutton, a Quaker who cofounded one of Britain's most prominent seed and garden-supply companies in 1806, confessed that he struggled with the same dilemma. The moment he got quiet, he admitted, his inner thoughts began pushing and shoving for attention. He heard the echoes of his own prayers, as well as his worries about the next day and his concerns about the day he was already living. He said he had to practice settling down in silence, which takes more than a little willpower, before he could open up to receive the Holy Spirit's whisper.[2] To Quakers like Sutton, silence itself is holy.

Most of the time my home doesn't have holy silence—instead, it is wholly noisy. Michael's friends like to stay for dinner and then spend the night strumming video game "guitars" that rock the speakers and vibrate the windows. With all the technology geeks in our family, we're constantly plugged into seven computers, four cell phones, five portable music players, and even a couple of old PDAs lying around. Until a battery dies, something is always chirping or beeping.

The best time for me to score any solitude is first thing in the morning, after I've poured my coffee but before I get dressed. There's an old recliner that I call my "prayer chair," a name my friend Mary came up with. It's the chair I rocked Michael in when he was a baby, so it's seen a fair share of spit-ups and spills, and its blue corduroy upholstery is worn at the edges where the dog used to enjoy scratching her back on it. It's been through so much, I think of it as a familiar, if rather shabby, friend. My homely chair sits in a corner of my bedroom, and I like to shut the door and plop down in it to read a psalm or devotional before I pray and listen for whatever God might want me to hear.

I also love my prayer chair because the cushions are soft and pillowy, and when I sink back in them, I can imagine God's arms wrapping around me as I pray. There's a lamp beside the chair, but I turn it off when I've finished reading so I can enjoy the restful darkness before the sun comes streaming through the bedroom windows. That's as close as I can get to what Jesus tells us to do: "When you pray, go into your [most] private room, and, closing the door, pray to your Father, Who is in secret" (Matt. 6:6 AMP).

According to Mark, that's what Jesus did too: "Very early in the morning, while it was still dark, He got up, went out, and made His way to a deserted place. And He was praying there" (Mark 1:35 HCSB).

Whether I can spend an hour or just a couple of minutes, my quiet time helps me center myself so I'm better equipped for the day. It helps me remember, when the noise starts to crank up around me, that I began my day with Jesus, and he hasn't left my side. It helps me find the kind of peace that David talked about in the psalms, when he said that he had cultivated a quiet heart and felt as contented as a baby rocked in its mother's arms (Ps. 131:2 MSG).

It can be tough to stay focused long enough to hear from God. Sometimes my mind feels like a radio with a dial spinning randomly from one station to another, and if you have a spouse who likes to click from one channel to another with the television remote, you know what that's like. I'm prone to start daydreaming about whether to cook a roast or enchiladas for dinner and then suddenly wonder if I was supposed to pick up a neighbor's child or shuttle the dog to the vet.

When my mind seems as cluttered as a closet, stuffed with yesterday's problems and tomorrow's fears, I get frustrated; but instead of giving up and getting up, I try to remember Saint Francis de Sales's advice to worshippers in the fifteenth century: "If the heart wanders or is distracted," he wrote, "bring it back to the point quite gently and replace it tenderly in its Master's presence. And even if you did nothing during the whole of your hour but bring your heart back and place it again in Our Lord's presence, though it went away every time you brought it back, your hour would be very well employed." It also helps to physically relax as I sit in silence, breathing deeply and slowly as I clear my mind and open my heart to God.

Not everybody can shut a door and spend time alone, of course. When we need more time in communion with God than we can squeeze out of our hectic lives, a retreat can help, like the one my friend John took a few years ago.

If you'd asked John to describe himself back then, he would have told you that he was living like a "corporate monk." *Corporate* and *monk* aren't words that usually go together, but when you hear John's story, you may identify with his situation. He's talking about being the kind of man who devotes long hours to his profession and who works tirelessly for others while making many personal sacrifices. A corporate monk, he would add, is a person who winds up spending long stretches of time by himself, without the companionship of family or friends.

John didn't expect to become a business-style monastic when he started his career more than fifteen years ago. He's a hardworking, intelligent guy who climbed the ladder of success in the hotel industry and was eventually rewarded with a management position and a top-notch salary. To most people, that sounds like the American dream.

But like most executive titles, John's came at a big cost. He found himself paying in the currency of too much stress and too many hours, managing ten different hotels in eight cities. Forced to relocate four times, he wound up repeatedly searching for new churches to attend. Because of his demanding schedule, meaningful relationships turned out to be the only things in John's life that he couldn't number. On that count, he was stuck at zero.

Feeling close to burnout, John decided to quit his job and accept another offer with a different company. He was hoping to renew the passion he'd once felt for his work, even though he was afraid he was rapidly turning into "the hardest-working, [most] people-pleasing, ambitious, white-collar mannequin you'd ever find," as he says.

Despite the job change, things kept going downhill. John's schedule got even crazier, and his new coworkers turned out to have what he calls a destructive and painfully unprofessional "eat-our-own mentality."

After eight months of madness, John had had enough. He resigned and walked away, but this time he didn't have another position in hand.

To give himself some space to figure out what God wanted him to do next, John signed up to take a spiritual retreat. His hope, as he says so beautifully, was to move closer "not only to my own purpose in life but to the God I'd grown so talented in distancing through my excuses and misaligned priorities.

"The hours and days to follow during my brief sabbatical touched upon areas of my life I'd conveniently avoided for years—listening, prayer, and silence," he says.

Like many other seekers, John stepped away from the noise of everyday life for a few days to seek God's will, hoping to find clarity and peace in silence. He didn't come back from the experience with a blinding revelation about the exact path his life should take, but John understands that life doesn't usually work that way. For most of us, finding the right direction can take time and patience, and often we hear from God in subtle ways, not spoken words.

"For me," John says, "it's a long and tedious road,"³ but it's one he's content to walk because he believes it will ultimately lead him to his true calling and to a deeper relationship with the God he loves so much.

It's a gutsy move, turning away from whatever keeps you attached to the world to immerse yourself in silence and prayer instead, because you never know ahead of time what God is going to reveal. He might ask you to keep on doing what you're doing but with a changed heart and a different attitude. He might send you in a completely new direction, and the unknown can be risky and scary. You may wind up making sacrifices you didn't foresee or leaving behind all that is comfortable and familiar.

Only one thing is sure: the world can be suffocating. Jesus wants us to have peace, and he knows how easily it eludes us. Before he made a feast for five thousand followers out of bread and fishes, he noticed how tired his disciples were. They'd been so busy doing his Father's work they hadn't even had time for a meal, and no doubt they were exhausted by the clamor from the crowds. "Come away by yourselves to a remote place and rest a while," Jesus told them (Mark 6:31 HCSB). His fellowship and peace would provide Living Bread for their souls.

Jesus is still giving us that wonderful invitation: come and spend some time with me. Shut your door. Turn your back on the crowds and distractions. Be quiet and still, and get to know me.

Silence has always been a companion to faith, and when we practice it, we're following the example of some of the Bible's best-known spiritual seekers.

Samuel nearly missed what God had to say to him until the old priest Eli told him to settle down. The Old Testament tells us that God seldom spoke or showed himself in those days, and his word was considered "rare and precious" (1 Sam. 3:1 AMP); so when young Samuel lay in his bed in the temple one night and heard someone calling him, he ran to see what the priest wanted. It wasn't me, Eli insisted. Go back to bed.

Samuel lay down in the darkness again, but again he heard a call. Back into Eli's chambers he went, and once more Eli packed him off to bed. When Samuel showed up in the doorway for a third time, Eli finally realized who was trying to get Samuel's attention.

"If the voice calls again," Eli told Samuel, "say, 'Speak, God. I'm your servant, ready to listen'" (1 Sam. 3:8–9 MSG). Samuel crawled back into his bed and waited expectantly. He had faith enough to believe that he would hear from the Lord, and he wasn't disappointed.

Eli realized that he could use Samuel's parading back and forth as one of those "teaching moments" that parents occasionally get. Most of us know we're supposed to communicate with God, and we spend our prayer time reciting our problems, listing our needs, and even offering up praise. But how often does somebody remind us that there's a time to stop talking and start listening?

It's true that God hasn't always revealed himself in silence. The Bible is filled with stories about how God has used spectacular and even cataclysmic events to catch our attention. God summoned Moses from the midst of a blazing bush, and to others he has announced his presence with thunder and lightning, thick clouds, or drenching rains. But we can miss him if we're looking only for the kind of drama we see in Hollywood movies.

Elijah discovered that God sometimes prefers to reveal himself in quiet ways. When Queen Jezebel threatened the prophet's life, Elijah ran away and crawled into a cave—and who hasn't longed to hide away in some dark place when things are going badly? God, take my life, he pleaded, ready to give up. But God made us to shine on hilltops, not cower in caves, and when he spotted Elijah, he demanded to know what the prophet was doing.

"I've been working my heart out," Elijah began, but now I've failed, he said, and my enemies want to kill me. Come out of that cave, God ordered, and "stand on the mountain at attention" (1 Kings 19:10–12 MSG).

When a superior officer passed by, soldiers stood at attention, and God seems to have told Elijah to snap to it, too, and get ready to obey his commands. But the word *attention* also means that God wanted the prophet to *pay attention* and focus on him, to concentrate on what he was saying and doing.

Apparently Elijah dragged his feet and didn't come out right away, because we're told that God proceeded to rake the mountain with hurricane-force winds. An earthquake split the ground, and fire crackled and roared. Yet God wasn't in any of these natural and noisy disasters. It was only when Elijah obeyed and slipped up to the mouth of the cave, into the fresh air and the sunshine, that he finally caught God's low, gentle whisper. There he found the strength and hope he needed.

Once, on a visit to Nevada, I drove into the desert because a friend had described to me its deep and lovely silence. After many miles of driving through a national park, I pulled off onto the shoulder, parked, and stepped outside. For a few minutes, all I heard was the hood of the car clicking and popping in the intense heat and the overflow of water from the air conditioner spattering onto the sand. I leaned against a boulder and waited for all the sounds to die down, and when they did, I spotted a tiny lizard at my feet and heard the faint noise he made as he skittered over a pile of pebbles. I listened to the wind soughing through a nearby rock formation. When a bird swooped by overhead, I heard the flutter of its broad wings. When nothing moved at all, my ears almost ached from the absence of sound, but I reveled in the rare and soothing peace, feeling that God was surely near.

The hush felt holy. I thought about Eli's words and repeated them silently to myself: *Speak, Lord. Your servant is listening.*

Seeds of Faith

Lord, teach me to be quiet and calm so I can hear what you are saying. Thank you for the peace we find in stillness. Thank you for helping me rest, knowing that you are faithful to watch over me always. Amen.

When life is heavy and hard to take,
go off by yourself. Enter the silence.
Bow in prayer. Don't ask questions:
Wait for hope to appear.
> *Lamentations 3:28–30 MSG*

Chapter 5

Your Turn to Talk

With every prayer and request,
pray at all times in the Spirit,
and stay alert in this, with all perseverance
and intercession for all the saints.
—EPHESIANS 6:18 HCSB

Are teenagers ever unplugged? If you're a parent, you know they're always connected to something: a portable music player, a cell phone, or a computer. My younger friends tell me that when they're texting, they can avoid all that time-wasting stuff like saying hello. With a wireless laptop, they can slump in the backseat of the car and fire off JPEGs to their buddies or post last night's party news while you drag them along on some boring family vacation.

Recently we met some old friends for dinner, and I had to laugh when I saw what our kids were doing. While they waited for the pizza to arrive, our teens—my son and their daughter—sat across the table from each other without exchanging a word. Meanwhile, under the cover of the white tablecloth, their thumbs were hammering the keys on their mobile phones. Seems they found that easier than actually talking (although having parents overhear their conversation might have had something to do with the choice of communication too).

If it sounds like I'm knocking the kids, I'm not. At their age I was holed up in my bedroom every night with a telephone glued to my ear, so it's only the technology that's different these days. That universal urge to keep up with your friends has stayed the same.

Even if you'd like to pull the plug sometimes, as we finally did before dessert arrived, the kids really do have it right. When there's a friendship at stake, you've got to stay in touch or you risk growing apart.

Most of us will experience times in life when we need to be quiet so we can hear God's voice, read his Word, and focus on him in love and adoration. Silence and meditation can calm our minds and expand our hearts. But there's also a time to speak up. That's what friends do, and amazingly, we *are* God's friends, thanks to Jesus. This is not high school or middle school, where we've got to wear the right clothes or have the best sneakers to be part of the group either. "No," Jesus says, "I've named you friends because I've let you in on everything I've heard from the Father. You didn't choose me, remember; I chose you, and put you in the world to bear fruit, fruit that won't spoil" (John 15:11–16 MSG).

How do we get to be friends with Jesus? He tells us we become his friends when we obey him. Another thing we must do is talk to God so that we keep the lines of communication open and stay fixed in his love.

Talking to God is as simple as whispering a prayer. Just as we break a nightlong fast with a morning meal—the literal meaning of *breakfast*—we can break a fast of silence with our prayers. Our words don't have to be eloquent; they can be as simple and direct as thanking him for the raisin bread in the toaster or the bus driver who delivers our children safely to school each day.

One thing we're warned not to do is to show off with flowery speeches that we're reciting from memory rather than from the sincerity of our hearts. When I get stuck for words, as I sometimes do, I've learned to turn to the psalms for help. These old and lovely words often petition God for the same things I need in my life today: protection, hope, healing, and forgiveness. I can read them aloud or simply look to them as a model. Sometimes the psalms spill over with gratitude for God's provision, as when David said, "I'm thanking you, God, from a full heart, I'm writing the book on your wonders. I'm whistling, laughing, and jumping for joy" (Ps. 9:1–2 MSG).

Other psalms are mournful and beseeching, filled with laments, and there have been hard times when those are the ones I've needed most to pray. Almost all of David's prayers were blunt, raw, and honest as he confessed to the same fears and doubts that all of us share. Over and over, the man who knew what it means to be hated and hunted down admitted his desperation and threw himself on God's mercy. On the run from enemies, he pled for a hiding place and turned to God for deliverance when he found himself in "deep, deep trouble again" (Ps. 31:6–13 MSG). Haven't we all been in trouble? Haven't we all wished for a safe place to run to?

At other times David was "doubled up with pain" (Ps. 22:1–2 MSG), calling for aid that didn't seem to come, until he started to question whether God cared. In his suffering, David challenged and even baited God, trying to provoke a response. Have you dumped me? he asked. Listen, God, he demanded, when the Ziphites tipped off Saul to David's hiding place, "Don't be too busy to hear me" (Ps. 54:1–2 MSG). David groaned and sighed; he soaked his bed with tears; he complained when deliverance didn't come as soon as he thought it should. Finally he was "reduced to a whine and a whimper, obsessed with feelings of doomsday" (Ps. 64:1 MSG).

Drenched pillows. Hoarse calls for help. Complaining and grumbling. It's startling when you discover that all these things describe a man who was dearly loved by God. When I first read David's words, I was surprised at how bitter and angry and even self-pitying he could sound. I never expected that the boy who had enough confidence to stand up to a giant would succumb to such dark thoughts. But it's that very darkness that speaks to us today and gives us the confidence to share our feelings with God, no matter what they are. David's honesty prompts us to be honest, too, knowing that God won't turn a deaf ear to anything.

I'm glad that the psalms, with all their marvelous complexity and humanity, aren't simply words of thanksgiving, even though it's so important to tell God how much we appreciate our blessings. It's a relief to know that he can handle hearing the worst that comes out of our hearts, that he doesn't want just neat, tidy packages of praise or old clichés that sound good but have lost their meaning through too much repetition.

The psalms have endured because they're packed with real, uncensored emotion and truth. It pleases God when we follow David's lead and confess the giants of fear and hopelessness and discouragement that we're up against because that demonstrates our trust in him, and he wants to help.

Prayer doesn't have to be pretty, but if we're going to have a good relationship with God, prayer does have to be constant. It needs to be real, and it's better still if we can pray with energy and passion. After all, John warns us in Revelation that God doesn't want a lukewarm relationship, where we're neither hot nor cold. He wants to encounter seekers who are impassioned, alive, and awake, such as David, and it's OK if we are imperfect. His goal is to get us to speak up and then to wait and listen until we are spoken to.

Nothing is too small and insignificant to bring to our heavenly Father. When children are little, they don't mind sharing every detail of their daily lives with their parents. We used to hear about the big kids who swiped a playground ball from Michael and his friends during recess or about how scary the substitute teacher was when she ordered the children to be quiet in the lunchroom. But around the time kids hit high school, the information highway shuts down. Parents still ask how things are going, but the answers always seem the same. Things are fine. The movie was fine. The math test was fine. The birthday party at a friend's house? You guessed it. Fine.

It's natural for a teen to pull back on some of that intimacy as he or she becomes more independent. But it's a disaster if we stop sharing our lives with our heavenly Father because prayer is a path that faith must walk.

When I was at my lowest point, I found myself unable to talk to God. I felt as if I'd prayed for help a thousand times, and as my troubles dragged on, I couldn't think of any more words to say. I'd gone to my knees and bowed my head until my mind went blank and my spirit felt as cold as stone.

What else is there to say? I wondered. I was tired and discouraged. Then one night, when my friend Martha phoned, I admitted to her how frustrated I was and how stale my prayers seemed to be. I told her I couldn't see any help on the horizon, and I couldn't even come up with any fresh words to say.

Martha has a gentle voice, and she spoke to me with kindness. "When we're worn out, it's hard to think straight," she said. "Why don't you let me say your prayers for you tonight? I'll do it while you rest. Let me take over for a while."

Her offer moved me to tears. I've had friends who prayed for me before, but no one had ever offered to actually say my prayers in my place so that I could put my head down and sleep, knowing my needs were continually being held up to

God at a desperate time. Martha did pray for me that night and many more, and it was a tremendous comfort until I was able to pick up my own prayers again. Since then, I've offered to hold others up when they were too tired to go on. It's a gift to have someone pray in your place.

Later, I remembered that I also had another friend who would pray for me. Jesus left us with a Comforter, the Holy Spirit, who does the same thing. The Message translation of Romans 8:26–28 beautifully describes the Spirit: "The moment we get tired in the waiting, God's Spirit is right alongside helping us along. If we don't know how or what to pray, it doesn't matter. He does our praying in and for us, making prayer out of our wordless sighs, our aching groans." The Spirit, as Paul assured us, "keeps us present before God" in much the same way Martha kept my needs lifted up to God during the night.

Max Lucado tells a wonderful story about finding his daughter Jenna, when she was six years old, standing in front of a mirror trying to peer down her own throat. She'd been told that God made his home in our hearts, so she was looking, she explained to her puzzled dad, to see whether he was really down there. Smart kid, checking in the right place, because the Bible tells us that the Spirit does indeed live in us, and he endlessly, tirelessly brings our concerns before God.

When we recover our own ability to pray, we don't take away from the Spirit's work. We simply add another dimension to our relationship with God. After my prayer break, I started small. Some of my prayers were for basic needs, and I prayed simply: "Please comfort Daddy in his grief." "Please send us more work." "Help" was all I could manage when I felt overwhelmed, but that was enough. I reminded myself that I was a child of God and that a loving father is willing and glad to supply what his children need.

I also set a goal to start praying all the time, without ceasing, as we're commanded to do, although I admit that I'll have to work at this for the rest of my life. Praying constantly sounds like an impossible task, but I've had to learn that prayer isn't just about a multitude of words. It can also be an ongoing connection to God that is wordless, a kind of attentiveness to what God is doing in our lives. We can cultivate a feeling of thankfulness when we're walking the dog on a cloudless day or picking up a spouse from the airport after she's had a safe flight home. We can breathe out gratitude for the uncle who calls on our birthday, the clean water that flows from a tap in our kitchens, the citrus-sharp taste of lemons, the teacher who draws a smiley face on our children's homework, or the medicine that makes us well.

God is everywhere, so we can speak a word to him when we're waiting for the kids to finish baseball practice or standing in line at the tag office or getting dressed for work every morning. We can pray for the people sitting across the room in the doctor's office or the politician whose face flashes on the television screen. One elderly lady tells me that she prays when she's scrubbing her dinner dishes at night, thanking God for the food that she's able to serve her family and grateful that she doesn't have to use "one of them [sic] noisy dishwashing machines."

Janet Holm McHenry, author of *PrayerWalk: Becoming a Woman of Prayer, Strength, and Discipline*,[1] likes to pray for each home she passes on her daily stroll around her neighborhood. I drive a lot more than I walk, unfortunately, so sometimes I turn off the radio when I'm in the car alone. That uninterrupted time is a great chance to say whatever is on my heart.

God welcomes us anytime we want to talk, whether we're mowing a lawn, changing a diaper, waiting on tables, or waiting for a business meeting. At its most fundamental, prayer can be an awareness that we're always with God and he is always with us, and our hearts can unfold before him as naturally and simply as a blossom opens. After all, God knows our thoughts before the words are on our tongues: "You know everything I'm going to say before I start the first sentence" (Ps. 139:1–6 MSG).

In the book of Luke, Jesus tells his disciples about a widow who wouldn't stop badgering a judge about her case. Her rights were being violated, she argued, and so she kept demanding justice. In Jesus' time, widows, especially those who didn't have sons, had very little power in society and had no one to speak up for them.

The judge, Jesus says, didn't worry about what God thought, and he cared even less about other people, but eventually the woman wore him out because she simply wouldn't leave him alone. She believed the judge had the power and ability to help her, and she was right. Faith and persistence won the day.

Jesus didn't mean, of course, that all we have to do is pray nonstop and we'll get everything we ask for. God promises to provide for our needs, but he isn't in the genie business of granting every idle wish. Instead, Jesus wanted us to know that God is like a judge because he is just and, ultimately, he can and will do what is right for us. Until he acts or reveals his will, we're supposed to keep praying. We're supposed to keep the conversation going.

When you can't figure out what to say, try what Jan Karon, the author of the delightful Mitford novels, calls the prayer that never fails: "Thy will be done."

Jan is someone who walks the talk. At almost fifty years old, she found herself aching to retire from the advertising career that had been her livelihood and try her hand at her childhood dream of writing. For two years she was steadfast in asking God for direction, and at long last, she says, she heard God's reply. She was to move forward, and she felt his promise to go with her.

Jan left her job to buy a small house in the mountains of North Carolina, where she pared her living expenses in half, bought a secondhand computer, and sat down to finally write her first book. And, as she has told interviewers, once she had the time and opportunity to write whatever she wanted, she went absolutely, completely bone dry. Not a single word crept out onto the page.

But Jan kept praying and believing and pinned her faith to Jeremiah 29:11, which is God's promise of a good plan for our lives. She hung on, getting by with freelance work for ad agencies, until the country fell into a severe recession and her earnings started to dwindle.

Even then Jan didn't give up. She continued putting her needs before God and watching for his guidance. As she lay in bed one evening, she says, an image of a man walking along a street popped into her mind. She got up and began to write his story.

When she had enough material in hand, Jan offered her work to an editor with the village newspaper, who began running it in weekly installments. For two more years she continued to crank out new stories, and then she spent an additional two years trying to place her manuscript, which had grown into a full-blown book. That's when a major publisher offered her a contract and turned her wonderful tales about Father Tim, an Episcopal priest, into a best-selling series about God's remarkable love.

Jan would probably be the first person to say that her financial and worldly success is beside the point. What really matters is that she stayed faithful in prayer. She took God at his word and literally believed his Word when he said he had a purpose for her life.

"When you call on me, when you come and pray to me," God says, "I'll listen" (Jer. 29:12 MSG). Once I overheard a boy trying to tell his dad a story about how much he liked riding his bike, and the dad, who was trying to navigate through a wicked traffic jam, shushed him. "Tell me later," he snapped. "I can't listen right now."

There is never a time when our heavenly Father won't listen. He longs for us to chatter away, to speak up, to praise him, to glorify him, and even to mope or gripe and whine, if that's what we need to do. Faith comes by hearing God's Word, but it's also strengthened and shared by speaking it.

Teenagers know they can plug in and connect anytime, anywhere. With God, so can we.

Seeds of Faith

Lord, I'm so glad I can talk to you about anything. Thank you for being the loving Father who always hears me. Amen.

May the words of my mouth
and the meditation of my heart
be acceptable to You,
LORD, my rock and my Redeemer.
Psalm 19:14 HCSB

Chapter 6

Getting Out
of the Desert

Do not remember the past events,
pay no attention to things of old.
Look, I am about to do something new;
even now it is coming. Do you not see it?
Indeed, I will make a way in the wilderness,
rivers in the desert.

—ISAIAH 43:18–19 HCSB

In certain wilderness areas you'd be wise to get some survival training before you go out hiking or camping on your own. Death Valley, for example, is a brutal place to visit despite its beautiful snow-capped mountains and multicolored rock formations. Some of the hottest temperatures on earth have been recorded there, and these badlands typically get less than two inches of rain a year. Rangers warn visitors to bring along plenty of extra drinking water, even if they're just driving through, because of the extreme risk of dehydration and heatstroke in the summer.

The Mojave Desert in Southern California gets a lot of traffic from nearby Las Vegas, but its hot, dry climate is pretty inhospitable too. Native Americans who lived in this high desert country traditionally used the barrel cactus for emergency "water" during prolonged droughts. If you've ever seen a barrel cactus, you know you'd have to be desperate to try hacking into one. The plant's Latin name is *Ferocactus*, and it's ferocious indeed. Barrel cacti have tough, ribbed skins covered with long, cruel spines that stab into skin like fishhooks. Even if you manage to get past the nasty barbs, you still have to pound, squeeze, or chew the slimy plant tissue inside to extract any moisture, and there's no guarantee it will really help. Although people have reportedly survived after drinking the juice from barrel cacti, the foul-smelling, bad-tasting liquid isn't a true substitute for water and can even be toxic.

Still, who wouldn't be tempted to try a sip under absolutely desperate circumstances? When the well goes dry, you'd better find a source of refreshment fast. No one and nothing can survive long without satisfying their thirst.

But surprisingly, not all deserts are made up of sand dunes and prickly plants, and there are other signs of thirst besides a dry mouth and weak knees. Sometimes we find ourselves wandering through desert places in our faith journey, too, living through periods when our spirits run dry rather than our bodies.

The Israelites literally traveled through the desert as Moses led them from Egypt toward the Promised Land. But they ran into the other kind of desert, too, when some of their scouts, who had gone ahead, reported that the land of Canaan was unconquerable, even though God had guaranteed to deliver it into their hands. As their faith evaporated under the scorching sun, God became angry. How long are you going to provoke me? he asked, until Moses interceded and asked God to turn his disappointment into forgiveness. God did pardon his wayward people, but their disbelief cost them dearly. They would never live in the land across the Jordan River; that privilege would belong to the next generation.

The rest of us don't have to put one foot out of our own front doors to wind up marching across the same kind of barren ground the Israelites trod. Deserts have been known to pop up in the middle of subdivisions and cities, on farms and fields, or anywhere faith begins to wither.

Fatigue and disappointment can turn hearts into dust bowls. Depression and sorrow sap joy and energy. It's not even necessary to experience a "full catastrophe," like the one experienced by novelist and Bible scholar Reynolds Price, when a battle with malignant spinal cancer left him partially paralyzed and confined to a wheelchair.[1]

A faith-drought can hit when nothing significant at all has happened. Some of us go through times when we still know God is there, but we feel as if we've lost our connection to him. Prayers stick in our throats, and we drag through graceless days and sleepless nights. The past seems scarred with missed opportunities, failed dreams, and broken promises. The future bristles with anxieties, fear, and worry. Just as the earth goes through seasons of drought and deluge, we can experience lack as well as abundance in our spiritual lives. Even the late Mother Teresa wrote numerous letters to her spiritual advisers, confessing an inability to sense or hear from God in her later years.

Part of the problem is depending too much on our feelings about God. I'd often heard that emotions aren't reliable, but I'd never really understood why until the day a suspicious test result from my annual physical left me sitting alone in a doctor's office. The test had suggested that I might have an illness with a genetic component, one I knew other members of my family had suffered, so I was worried as I waited for the specialist to come in.

When the doctor arrived, she repeated the test and left to read the results. Twenty minutes passed, while I broke out in a sweat. The door banged open, and she came in, frowning, to announce that the test was inconclusive. We'd have to do it again.

Another twenty minutes ticked past, and, unbelievably, she reappeared with the same grim news. The results weren't clear, so we needed to repeat the test once more. She left, and now a half hour elapsed. My heart began to thud until I felt it through my chest. My blouse, damp with perspiration, began sticking to my clammy skin. *Why didn't I bring a friend with me?* I wondered, forgetting that Jesus, my best Friend, was always near. I got up and looked at myself in a mirror hanging over a small sink. My face was getting beet red as my blood pressure rose.

I have this terrible disease, I thought. *They've done this test four times now, so they are looking to see how far it's progressed. I have it. I just know it.*

By the time the doctor finally returned, I was light-headed and breathless. I waited for her to say I needed treatment. I felt it coming. I was sure.

And I was wrong.

"You're fine," she said breezily. "You can go."

It was so anticlimactic, I had to ask her to repeat herself. "Thank you, God," I whispered, as I practically raced for the door.

I don't fault myself for a lack of faith this once—although I've dropped the ball plenty of other times—because there is a chance I'll have to face this disease one day. That's a reality of living in a physical, fallen world. But the experience taught me a powerful lesson about how easily we can be misled by our own feelings. I'd been convinced I had a health problem, but I was mistaken. Fear and anxiety had tricked me and led me to the wrong conclusion. Similarly, if we don't feel God's presence, that doesn't mean he's absent. Emotions aren't trust-worthy, but he is.

God keeps his promises, but we have to guard our hearts and stay out of those deserts of unbelief. So what are we supposed to do when faith threatens to slip away like sand pouring between our fingers?

Jesus gave us one answer, although it sounds, at first, like a paradox: we can help someone else, and in doing so, we help ourselves. Service—reaching out to people in need—is a wonderful way to approach God and refresh that divine connection. Jesus taught his followers to "Give, and it will be given to you; a good measure—pressed down, shaken together, and running over—will be poured into your lap" (Luke 6:38 HCSB). The Message translation sums it up: "Giving, not getting, is the way" (Luke 6:38 MSG).

A group of people living on the Blue Hill, Maine, peninsula know what it means to serve. More than a decade ago, about sixty residents of this New England community came together to form a free-of-charge, all-volunteer group called Neighborcare. Not everyone shares the same spiritual beliefs, but each volunteer has a heart for helping. Their goal is to give joyfully to any sick or ailing neighbor, whether they're called to listen compassionately when a wife grieves over her husband's passing or water a sick gardener's houseplants or stack firewood and shovel snow for someone who is handicapped and housebound. If we're people of faith, our acts of love and charity speak volumes about God as we obey the command to treat others as we want to be treated. We can be an oasis in their deserts, offering the drink of Living Water that is Jesus.

Every person has a different gift for service, and you don't have to be ordained to do God's work; ordinary will do just fine. My former coworker M. A. honors God when she pulls off the highway to coax stray dogs out of danger and into her car. Her ministry is combing the burrs out of each animal's ragged coat, feeding it until its skinny ribs disappear, and finding it a safe and loving home.

Dads serve when they coach soccer teams and build kids up with positive words instead of cutting them down with sharp ones. An elderly woman who is too feeble to drive anymore serves when she mails out cards to people in her community who are bedridden or lonely or unemployed. All of us are witnesses when we let our hurts and wounds transform us instead of destroying us so that we can turn around and comfort someone else.

My longest stretch in the desert began when my mother died. Like Reynolds Price, I slammed into a personal catastrophe and found my beliefs tested when Bill's layoff went on and on and my father fell into a chasm of grief and suffering. Each morning I got out of bed and felt as if I'd picked up despair and slung it like a weight on my back. Hope, which comes from God, felt more and more like a mirage in the distance, something I might never have again.

For months after the accident that shattered my shoulder, the only way I could find relief from pain was to lean back in my old recliner, my prayer chair. I spent many frustrating days unable to work at my desk or even around the house. Without help, I couldn't tie my shoes, cut the food on my plate, or wash my hair. I needed assistance to bathe, and getting dressed was a daily struggle. I couldn't drive at all.

I couldn't do much of anything, actually, except pray, so that's what I did. I prayed a lot. I began to ask God what I was supposed to do next, and as Scripture verses popped into my head, I started to come up with some answers.

One thing quickly became apparent: I was missing a relationship with other believers and not just because I hoped someone would stop by to help me make a sandwich at lunchtime or sweep my kitchen floor. Because we had slacked off in going to church when our lives went sour, I had slowly and almost imperceptibly become isolated, and that isolation, I realized, was partly to blame for my parched spirit. We are meant to be that cord of many strands that Ecclesiastes talks about because left alone we often become weak and vulnerable. When we have companionship on our faith walk, we're less likely to wander off into the wilderness.

Everyone needs stamina and support to endure a long journey. Every Fourth of July, runners race down the closed-off streets in Atlanta to compete for fame and prizes in the Peachtree Road Race, the world's largest ten-kilometer race. Friends and fans line the roadsides as the runners pass, holding out water bottles for them to grab so they can slake their thirst without missing a beat. It's a grueling race in Atlanta's sweltering heat and humidity, and the athletes need to drink plenty of water to make it to the finish line.

The rest of us need plenty of Jesus to make it to our finish lines. He promised the Samaritan woman at the well that he could supply her with all the water she'd ever need, through his grace.

I needed God when I broke my shoulder—I will always need him—and sometimes I think slipping on my kitchen floor that morning was a pretty good thing, after all, because it literally and figuratively brought me to my knees. The hours I spent in that old recliner gave me time to see how far I'd wandered away from a company of fellow believers and how little service I was giving to others.

I wanted out of my desert, so I made some changes. I'd stopped going to Bible-study groups, but I started attending again. I took my various Bible translations off my bookshelves and began to really study and absorb them. Grateful for the friends who brought me dinner or drove me to doctors' appointments, I promised God I'd actively look for ways to serve others when I was on my feet again. That wasn't just the right thing to do; I wanted to help as an act of praise and worship, knowing that God is delighted when we grow a servant's heart.

We resumed our attendance at church, too, so we could continue to find refreshment for our lives. Sometimes we attended the morning service, which offered a traditional form of worship, but we also discovered a wonderful, outside-the-box contemporary service called The Well. Led by our associate pastor, John, in a casual, coffeehouse-style setting in our fellowship hall, it overflows with exciting, new ways to adore God and experience him.

Worshippers at The Well sing contemporary Christian songs and watch multimedia presentations as a church leader speaks. We might split into small groups and sit around tables while we make a collage about a Bible story or compose our own prayers on a computer that projects them onto the wall for everyone to read. John has given us religious meditations by poets like T. S. Eliot to read, and he's invited modern dancers to perform and interpret the gospel for us. We've had question-and-answer sessions about events and people in the Bible, and nothing is off limits as we explore God's Word together.

We've even shared the U2charist, an innovative Communion service that uses spirit-flavored music by the Irish rock band known as U2. The U2charist, which was inspired by lead singer/songwriter Bono's Christian faith, seems to have started with a church in Maine. Thanks to the Internet, this type of contemporary worship has spread to Protestant churches like ours, where it's reaching many believers who have drifted away from more formal services. Admittedly, worshipping in jeans and sitting around candlelit tables while you sip coffee and soak up the Word isn't for everybody, but it is a very real source of refreshment and energy for many people who find traditional praise too "dry." Like a fountain, The Well bubbles over with the life-giving Word of God, and it seems to fit in beautifully with Paul's words to Timothy: "Let's see how inventive we can be in encouraging love and helping out, not avoiding worshiping together as some do but spurring each other on" (Heb. 10:24 MSG).

Getting Out of the Desert

Deserts can be lonely, desolate places, without any grasses for animals to graze or pools of water to fill empty canteens or leafy trees to provide rest and shade. But even deserts can bloom.

In the Sonoran Desert of Arizona, huge carpets of colorful wildflowers appear every few years. Scientists don't know exactly what sparks these rare bursts of blooms, although they think it's some combination of the right soil and temperature. Nothing happens, though, until seasonal "triggering rains" arrive to nudge the long-dormant seeds to sprout. When the right elements combine, the ground explodes into a brilliant tapestry of bright blue lupines, gold and scarlet poppies, and purple owl clover. Cacti unfold their exotic blossoms, adding to the show.

When these great sweeps of flowers blossom, the landscape is transformed. They are proof that beauty can be born even in desert places. All it takes is life-giving water.

When we drench ourselves in the goodness of God's perfect love, when we pour ourselves out in joyful service and join a community of fellow believers, we can be transformed too. We can walk confidently through our wilderness places because he has promised, "I will cause showers to come down in their season; they will be showers of blessing" (Ezek. 34:26 NASB).

We may endure a season in the desert, but God has guaranteed it: in due time the rain will come.

Seeds of Faith

God, when our spirits become dust-dry, refresh us. Show us how to help others. Bind the strand of each individual life into a cord of strong and lasting fellowship. Let our hearts overflow with your amazing love! Amen.

God—you're my God! I can't get enough of you!
I've worked up such hunger and thirst for God,
traveling across dry and weary deserts.
So here I am in the place of worship, eyes open,
drinking in your strength and glory.
In your generous love I am really living at last!
My lips brim praises like fountains.

Psalm 63:1–4 MSG

Chapter 7

Digging Deep

May your roots go deep into the soil of God's marvelous love. . . .
—EPHESIANS 3:17 TLB

It's taken me ten years, but I think I've finally made a break-through. This summer my garden was the best it has ever been. My tomato plants grew so tall they spilled over the tops of their wire cages and dangled glossy, red fruit that looked like Christmas-tree ornaments from almost every branch. My eggplants fattened up into enormous, purple pears, yet they remained soft and tender enough to stew up in a pot of delicious ratatouille. The cucumber vines stretched and sprawled across the yard, studded with future pickles for my pantry shelves, while sprigs of basil, dill, and mint outside my kitchen multiplied until I could smell their spicy fragrance through the open windows.

Our harvest had never been this abundant before, and I blame most of the problem on our dirt. The part of Georgia I live in is cursed with red clay, which is a sorry excuse, as my grandmother used to say, for soil. When the stuff gets wet, you can pick up a handful, squeeze it into a ball, drop it on the ground, and it won't shatter. In other words, when it rains, our ground turns into a thick goo that plant roots can't penetrate.

We don't fare any better in dry weather. Once red clay loses its moisture, it takes on the consistency of hardened cement. Even the sharpest shovel bounces off, forcing us to grab a pickax and start swinging. One summer, when Bill was trying to dig out the foundation for a new garden shed, he actually resorted to borrowing a friend's jackhammer to break up the ground.

I figured out long ago that if I wanted to grow anything in this dirt, I'd have to amend it; so for almost a decade I've been adding composted eggshells and coffee grinds, vegetable scraps, leaf mold, and manure. We've dumped in bags of sand and peat moss, and we've hoed and shoveled, tilled and dug, until finally the clay has loosened up. We've even been able to raise some nice root crops like beets and carrots, which usually protest poor growing conditions by growing lumpy and gnarled.

Of course, more sensible people can't always understand why we're willing to put so much effort into our yard. One afternoon a friend came by to visit and found me struggling to pull some weeds encroaching on a row of green beans. She sat on an overturned pail to watch as I chopped at a stubborn patch of crabgrass and, because we hadn't had any rain in a while, raised a cloud of choking red dust into the air.

She coughed and shook her head. "Look at you," she scolded, and I glanced at the dirt smeared on my sweaty arms and legs. "You can buy tomatoes at the grocery store for a couple of dollars. Why are you working so hard out here?"

If you've ever eaten a juicy, homegrown tomato, still warm from the sun, you know the answer to her question. She thought she was making a good point. Gardening is a lot of work, and yes, you can buy the same things without spending a lot of money. But that didn't mean I was going to stop digging, because my mouth was already watering for those delicious summer fruits and veggies, and I knew that if I kept at it, my labor would pay off. I'd be able to go outside every afternoon and fill a basket with the fresh food I'd grown. That would make all the grime and sweat worthwhile—even if we did have to jackhammer the yard sometimes.

To tell you the truth, once it was almost as hard for me to believe in God as it was to dig in that red Georgia clay. I had to do a lot of work to get down to the fundamentals of what I really knew about him. I had been taught to believe that he would help us when we called on him, but what was I to think when a godly friend retired and died of a heart attack just as he was supposed to start enjoying his so-called golden years? Where was God when a teenage boy in our community, despondent over a breakup with his girlfriend, chose to end his young life? I'd been raised to believe in God, but as I went through trials of my own and saw so much suffering in the world around me, I began to wonder whether I really knew him at all.

Some nights I'd sit on our back deck and try to pray in the darkness. More than once, I stormed outside after a bad day—and so many days were bad back then—and yelled, "Where are you, God?" into the woods behind our house.

Nowadays I look back and think I was behaving the way Michael used to when he was two years old. Parents talk about the terrible twos, and that can be a rough age. Sometimes when I had to discipline Michael, he'd ball up his small fists, prop them on his hips, and stand there to defy me. *No* was his favorite word, which made me want to swat his little bottom, and I'd have to stop and remember that he was just a toddler and had a lot to learn. I recognized that some of his misbehavior was more about his own frustration than anything else. He got mad and disobeyed when he couldn't do what he wanted, like scramble up the dangerously steep basement steps alone or pedal his tricycle down the road just as tired drivers were speeding home from work.

I didn't hear anything from God when I yelled at him from the back deck, but secretly, I sure wanted to. Like Michael when he was a baby, I was frustrated and stymied by my unanswered prayers, stuck in what seemed like a hopeless situation. I was also distraught that none of us had been able to help my father, who felt so lost and miserable after my mother's death. In short, I was blaming God and was really mad at him.

To try to make sense of what was happening, and to blow off steam, I started scribbling in a journal, hoping to see some shape or pattern emerge from what was going on in my life. Most people seem able to bear even great trouble if they can find some purpose or meaning in it, and I was no different.

One evening, I sat up long after Bill and Michael went to bed and watched a program on public television about the late author and professor Joseph Campbell. Campbell had done a series of fascinating interviews about mythology with reporter Bill Moyers, and because I'm a writer, the program caught my attention when the men started to discuss how stories are created.

As the hour ticked away, I realized that Campbell was talking about the Bible as a collection of myths intended to explain the world around us, and he did not see it as a divine revelation. With a sinking heart, I heard him add that although he'd been raised a Roman Catholic, his studies and experiences had led him to believe that God was only a word or a kind of metaphor that people used for something we can't see or understand. He did not believe in a personal God who cared for us, he said. I felt my face flush as I listened, as if I'd been searching for answers, and here they were, broadcast into my very own living room. They just weren't the answers I'd hoped for.

I turned off the TV and sat there alone for a while, letting his theories sink in. I was discouraged and depressed, and his words took root in my heart like something ugly and twisted, like weeds that strangle anything good that is trying to grow.

Maybe Campbell had it right, I thought miserably. God made the world, but now he was too busy to know and care about every moment of one small life. After all, I reasoned, did it really matter to God if a high-school team prayed for a win before a football game? Was he listening when the local garden club asked for rain to make a few silly little flowers grow? Was he sorry when my sister's beloved dogs jumped the fence and ran away? I remembered something my friend Martha said years ago when she was carrying her little boy and one of his shoes fell off and was lost in a huge parking lot. As her husband went back to search for the missing sneaker, she prayed that God would help him find it, and that had surprised me. Praying for a toddler's shoe? I'd gone to church all my life, but I'd never heard of such a thing. Somehow I'd come to think that prayer was about the big stuff in life, like war and disease or floods and famine—but one small shoe? I didn't understand it back then, and when I heard what Campbell was saying, I decided I must have been right in the first place. God was too big for our daily, ordinary concerns. He had spun the world off into the void and stepped back, taking his hands off our petty lives. Only that would explain why there was so much suffering.

No, I told myself, sitting in the dark room, alone with my wounded heart. God was impersonal, if he was at all. Maybe he was another ancient myth, as Campbell suggested. I turned on a lamp and got out my journal, filling page after page with my questions and black thoughts.

Over the next few days, I turned the pages into an essay and sent it in to the local newspaper, which ran an article every week on a different aspect of faith. I bled all over that essay, admitting that the troubles my family had faced were eating away at everything I'd once believed.

It was sad, dark stuff, but my gut was churning. The hole of doubt I was falling into seemed bottomless.

I'm sorry now I wrote that bitter essay. I'm not proud that I questioned God when things got really tough for the first time in my life. I've met Holocaust survivors who stood strong, while I stumbled and fell flat on my face. But the truth is the truth, and until we're honest with ourselves, we probably won't be honest with God either. You can't lie to a friend and expect to have a good relationship, and it's the same with Jesus, who is our steadfast Friend. As pastor and author Rick Warren has said, pride tempts us to hide our faults and sins, to try to persuade everybody that our lives are going great and we're always in control.[1] It's hard to admit it when we're wrong, but I was wrong, and I'm sorry for my lapse of faith.

Sadly, my experience isn't unique. The psalmists also poured their hearts out to God, and he listened and accepted their blunt honesty. Their works are filled with sorrow and longing, despair and pleading, and they often asked God, Have you forgotten me? How long must I wait for deliverance? Where are you, anyway? It's not a far stretch to think they also shouted into the darkness behind their homes.

I thought I'd been waiting a long time for God to reply to me, and my hope had run out. But God had the timing in hand, and help was on its way to me as soon as the essay appeared.

Recently our associate pastor, John, talked about God's timing. "God always shows up at the right time," he reminded us, even though his schedule may be different from ours. Sometimes God waits until what feels like the eleventh hour, when our backs are against the wall, and he's the only hope we have left. We can't say for sure why he waits to answer sometimes, but we can say this: even if God is our last hope, he's also our best hope.

When my essay ran in the paper, an amazing thing happened. People who read it started writing to me that very morning, using an anonymous e-mail address the editor had asked me to include. By lunchtime that day, I had more than a hundred messages waiting on my computer.

One after the other, I opened the e-mails and read them until my eyes blurred with tears. Each repeated the same encouragement: Hold on. God is real. God loves you and will help. Forget that impersonal nonsense, they said, since I had written about the Campbell interview. No matter what happens, no matter what the most respected author or professor says, God is with you. He's in control, and he is trustworthy.

It took days, but I replied to each person. The majority of the e-mails sounded like mini-sermons, and I wrote back politely, though I secretly dismissed their messages. I was incredibly grateful for the kindness that prompted the senders, but I was too far gone by then to absorb what sounded like preaching. Still, all the e-mails touched me deeply. God was sending me some powerful testimonies at my eleventh hour, but I was resisting. Little did I know how much help was already on the way.

Over the next week or two, most of my e-mail correspondents dropped away. I understood; I certainly hadn't expected complete strangers to stay in touch.

But surprisingly, one woman did keep in touch. A couple of times each week, her e-mails popped up to say she was praying for me. Sometimes she simply said, "Hang on. I've been through tough times, too, and God is faithful." Her messages were water to my thirsty spirit. I began turning on my computer every morning just in hopes of hearing from her. She was never preachy or strident, which is probably why her words left such an impression on me. I wasn't open to hearing much more at that time, but I was hungry for comfort and hope. Her e-mails kept coming, week after week, brimming with kindness and gentle reminders that God is good.

Months went by, and we began to really "talk." She let me pour out my troubles in my e-mails, and she didn't judge me. After a while, I trusted her enough to reveal my real name. We started to share tidbits about our children, our work, our husbands and homes. Eventually we exchanged addresses, and she began to drop letters into the mail for me. She sent me a picture when her son got married, and I put it on my refrigerator so I could look at the friend I'd never met but had come to love and admire.

God was working in my life, and I could feel it, feel the friendship this stranger was extending to me when I felt so alone and bereft. My circumstances were not getting better, so I was struggling to hold my tattered faith together. But my new friend kept in touch, and something in my heart started to wake up again. I began carrying the notes she mailed me around in my purse so I could dash off to a ladies' room and read them if I was out somewhere and felt the need for encouragement. The Bible verses she sent were warming my heart and lifting my spirits: "I know what I am planning for you. . . . I have good plans for you, not plans to hurt you. I will give you hope and a good future" (Jer. 29:11 NCV). "The LORD is my Shepherd; I shall not want" (Ps. 23:1 KJV).

I'm praying for you and your family, she wrote. I couldn't believe how much compassion one stranger could show to another. *What must God be like,* I wondered, *if someone I'd never met could take me under her wing to shelter and comfort me?* I began to realize that I was seeing Jesus' reflection in my e-mail friend, and that awed me. I wanted to know this loving Father. I wanted to know this Jesus. Slowly I was climbing out of the hole I'd fallen in, finding my way back into the light.

My friend won't take credit for helping me dig deep and find my faith again. When I tell people about her, she asks me not to reveal her name, preferring to give any glory to God, and I respect that.

It's been about seven years since we started corresponding, and we've still never met. But I'm sure I'd recognize her heart anywhere, and I'm still amazed and filled with gratitude that God let our paths cross when my faith was nearly gone. I thought God was silent, and I interpreted that as rejection or abandonment. But God was there all along, and in his perfect timing he sent help when I was truly ready to receive it. And he used e-mails and a computer; some note cards and stamps; and one remarkable, loving, generous woman who walks in his footsteps.

Once Jesus told a parable about a man who sowed seeds. Some of the seeds went astray and were nibbled up by birds. Others were scattered onto rocks, where they sprouted but quickly perished because they had no water. Still more seeds fell into thorns that choked them before they could grow. But finally, some of the seeds landed on good soil, and they stretched their tender, green shoots toward the sky and flourished.

Plants can't grow in hard, dry ground, and love can't grow in hardened hearts. We have to be open and receptive to catch the seeds—the Word of God—if his spirit is going to grow in our lives and produce a bountiful harvest.

Even when failure and loss and pain block our path, we can still dig into the Scriptures and see what they say about our Creator. If the stony soil of our hearts needs loosening, we can bring the tools of prayer and faith and the Holy Spirit into our gardens.

Getting your faith back once it has gone missing isn't easy. But be absolutely sure of this: the God who made us knows how to help us. Once we're ready to receive his gifts, he will renew and restore. Then he promises, "Blessed is the man who trusts me . . . the woman who sticks with God. They're like trees replanted in Eden, putting down roots near the rivers— never a worry through the hottest of summers, never dropping a leaf, serene and calm through droughts, bearing fresh fruit every season" (Jer. 17:7–8 MSG). With that sweet assurance, how could any gardener ask for more?

Seeds of Faith

Heavenly Father, thank you for planting your mercy and grace in our lives. Nourish our faith and help it grow in the fertile soil of our willing hearts. Amen.

---

*"The seed is the Word of God . . . the seed in the good earth—
these are the good-hearts who seize the Word and hold on
no matter what, sticking with it until there's a harvest."*

Luke 8:11–15 MSG

Chapter 8

Looking for God Signs

*How great are his signs,
how mighty his wonders!*
—DANIEL 4:3 NIV

Amy Blackmarr was staring idly at her computer screen one morning, she says, when she had a revelation. She was thirty-three years old at the time, the owner of a successful paralegal business in Kansas, when she suddenly realized how fast another thirty years could slip by before she had a chance to do all the things she really wanted to. She'd never had time to sit down and really write, for example. That's why, just eight months later, Amy found herself selling her business and loading her computer and books, a library card, and some long underwear into her pickup truck for a long drive back to her family's farm in Georgia.

Getting back to your roots might sound appealing, but don't imagine that Amy went home to some kind of Southern mansion draped in moonlight and magnolias. Instead, she moved into an old fishing shack her late grandparents had built beside a pond on their property. Her new residence wasn't much more than a tin-roofed "scarecrow" of a cabin, as Amy says, with tar-paper walls and sloping floors, and it sat surrounded by some eighty-odd acres of pine trees, sweet gums, and wild grapevines. The cabin didn't have hot water or central heating (which explains why Amy needed long underwear even in south Georgia). It was a pretty isolated setting for a young woman unless you count the stray dogs that kept turning up, an occasional neighbor who dropped by, and the baby rattlesnakes that liked to nest under Amy's porch.

It should be clear by now that Amy wasn't obsessed with having a high-paying career or the fancy material trappings that come with it. Like that old tax protestor Thoreau, she deliberately left her comfortable existence behind for a chance to figure out what really mattered in life and found the peace and beauty of the old farm calling to her.

When you read Amy's wonderful essays, published in a collection called *Going to Ground: Simple Life on a Georgia Pond*, you can see how her new lifestyle helped her connect to the natural world.[1] During the five years she lived on her grandparents' land, Amy listened to concerts sung by squeaky frogs and watched in delight as the chinaberries and cherry trees bloomed. She boiled water for showers and searched for arrowheads to add to her collection, wrote in her journal and learned to cook a gamey-tasting squirrel stew. Because she understood that nature isn't always lovely or kind, she also endured swarms of stinging yellow flies each summer, and because she couldn't get rid of them anyway, she learned to tolerate the noisy band of white-footed mice that danced behind the cabin walls at night.

Amy also went out looking for what she calls "God sign." A sign, as any good tracker knows, is some sort of evidence that a person or an animal has been around. If you're hunting for deer, your sign might be hoofprints in the damp sand beside a stream. Gnawed bark on a tree could signal that beavers are nearby, building a dam. A patch of flattened grass at your feet might indicate that fox kits slept there the night before.

Other signs are harder to spot, so you've got to pay close attention or you'll overlook them. Serious trackers bring out dogs to "go to ground," which means that the hounds put their noses to the dirt to sniff out a trail. When you're out searching for something or someone and you find signs, you can feel confident that you're not wasting your time; you're headed in the right direction. What you're looking for really is out there, maybe just around the next bend, and if you stay the course, you'll find whatever it is that you're seeking.

During the years Amy spent at the farm, she occasionally went out looking for signs of God. She wasn't expecting to find the same kind of physical evidence you'd find after an animal has lumbered through the woods. As she says, our minds are too small to get a fix on the infinite and eternal, and we can't pin the Creator down to the limits of time and space. But Amy also understands that just because you can't see something or touch it with your hands, that doesn't mean it isn't there. Thoreau saw the Divine in nature when he lived in the woods near

Walden Pond, and Amy imagines she's seen it, too, in the way hawks glide on columns of warm, rising air or in the watercolor wash of a lavender and blue sunset.

God has left his handprint in every corner of creation. While I'm awed by his majestic mountain peaks and vast, green oceans, I also see his signature in small things. I fancy that pearls hiding in homely oyster shells are signs of his playfulness, along with the crayon-bright colors of butterfly wings. I see his eye for detail in the honeybees that pollinate our avocados and almonds, in the pungent smells of chrysanthemums and marigolds, and in the spicy bite of onions and peppers. To me, God proves his presence in microscopic organisms that scientists see underneath their scopes, in the earthworms that aerate my garden soil, and in the invisible air that trees breathe out and we breathe in.

Poets, writers, and artists have always had a keen eye for little things that point us toward great faith. Who would have thought to thank God for spots and dabs of color? Gerard Manley Hopkins did. The Jesuit priest and poet praised "dappled things," like the mottled blues and whites of the sky, the rosy freckles on trout, and the tawny streaks on a cow's hide. In *The Color Purple*, a novel by Alice Walker, the character Shug says God basks in our admiration and loves to share the good things he's created, such as a field of purple wildflowers.

Annie Dillard, the author of the Pulitzer Prize–winning *Pilgrim at Tinker Creek*, also recorded glimpses of the Creator while living and working near Virginia's Blue Ridge Mountains.[2] She set out, she says, to become an "explorer" and a "stalker" on a hunt for wonder, whether romantic or rough. She found it, too, in the maple seeds that helicoptered out of the trees overhead and in the water striders she watched as they tiptoed across a stream without ever breaking the water's surface. It takes a marvelous God to put so much attention into his design.

When doubts try to overshadow my faith, I go outside to look for my own God signs, and it's the natural world that reassures me that he is real and near.

Sue Monk Kidd had already found success writing Christian books and magazine articles when she slammed into a spiritual crisis in midlife and also went looking for God in the physical world. There was a time, she confesses in her book *When the Heart Waits: Spiritual Direction for Life's Sacred Questions,* that her life seemed to have lost its meaning, becoming as dreary as the February skies over her South Carolina home.[3] Her marriage, she admits, had turned stale, and the religion that had sustained her for many years began to feel suffocating. One cold day, she wandered outside for a walk and bowed her head against the harsh wind, perhaps bowing her heavy heart, too, as she tried to figure out what to do.

As she strolled underneath a dogwood tree, Kidd says, something dangling from a bare limb caught her eye. She looked up to see a wrinkled, brown cocoon.

Ms. Kidd stopped. Was God trying to get her attention? She wondered whether the cocoon was a sign that she should wait patiently for her life to unfold, as the caterpillar inside was patiently waiting to hatch as a new and different creature. Carefully she snapped the twig and carried the cocoon home, where she attached it to a tree in her yard. Throughout the winter and into spring, she watched, until the chrysalis burst open and revealed a newborn butterfly. She taught herself to wait and watch until God gave her direction in both her personal life and her spiritual journey.

I've had my own faith crisis, and I know what it feels like to go through a bleak season. One day while I was struggling, Sandy, who was still serving as our associate pastor at the time, took me to lunch at a Chinese restaurant and listened as I poured out my doubts and fears. We sat in a room decorated with cheerful red paper banners and painted dragons as silverware clinked and diners chattered happily around us. While I drank cups of bitter, hot tea that matched the bitterness in my soul, I admitted that I was mad at God for my mother's suffering and death, and then my father's, and for all the other trouble that had come my way. I remember putting down the teacup and blowing my nose on a paper napkin while tears welled in my eyes.

When I finished, Sandy nodded and spoke words of comfort to me. "It's OK. God can handle our anger and hurt. He knows what to do with disbelief. Just keep talking to him."

After I washed my face and went to bed that night, I lay awake, as I often did, and remembered our conversation. Sandy had also reassured me that God answers our prayers—always:

"He may not answer the way we want or expect, but he will do what is right and what is best. We might not see it that way, because his answers aren't always easy. But he does answer."

I punched my pillows a lot during those restless nights, and I prayed. Show up, I asked God again and again. I'm sinking here. Please, just show up. We need some help right now, and I can't see any evidence that you're at work. In fact, I can't see you at all.

My faith was a carnival ride back then, climbing up one day and plummeting the next, depending on whether I'd had a good day or a bad one. If I'd been to the cemetery to take flowers or had yet another bill that seemed impossible to pay, I felt forsaken. If I'd been to church, I felt encouraged. But God didn't indicate he'd heard me. Life slogged on as before. Nothing happened.

That is, nothing seemed to be happening.

Then one day I drove home from the grocery store after stocking up with milk and laundry detergent and other necessary items that stretched our thin budget even further. I hated shopping, which meant thinking about money and work, which were always in short supply. When a commercial started blaring on the radio, I turned it off, irritated by the cheerful song that seemed to mock my messed-up life. My nerves were frayed.

Just ahead, a traffic light blinked from green to red, so I slowed down and stopped. Impatient to get home, I tapped my fingernails on the steering wheel and sighed, trying to empty my mind of negative thoughts.

Suddenly two words flashed through my head. *Stop struggling.*

I didn't actually hear them; whatever was in my head was not an audible voice. I can't say that I have ever heard God speaking audibly to me. Yet immediately I felt that he was telling me what he wanted me to do. I was supposed to stop blindly flailing in every direction against "fate" and just let go. If I wanted peace, if I wanted help, I had to trust that God knew what to do and when. No more worrying about the checkbook or a job. No more asking, Where are you? No more demanding, Are you there? No more anger and no more fear.

If we went bankrupt, we were to go bankrupt. If the car broke down in the middle of the road, then the car broke down. If someone got sick, they would be sick. We could work hard, or we could walk, or we would look for a doctor. But we were not able to change the outcome of anything. Only God was, and the only solution to every single question or problem was to trust him.

The Bible had been telling me to pay attention to what I was doing each day and to keep my grasping little hands off tomorrow, and I finally understood.

And amazingly, after literally years of trying to lean on God's grace and mercy—trying so hard to figure out how a person does that—I did it. I just did it. In that very moment, I surrendered.

It felt as if a rubber band wrapped around my chest had unexpectedly popped off. All the stress and anxiety and doubt that left me feeling wound up and tense were gone. There was no more effort on my part. It was like letting go of the string of a balloon you've been holding for a long time and seeing the balloon lift into the sky and disappear.

I'd known all along that I had the wrong attitude because my fears were running my life, and fear is not from God. Fear is the weapon the enemy uses against us. Fear, not doubt, is the very opposite of faith. I'd asked God to forgive my lack of belief, and I wanted to trust him. I really did. I just hadn't been able to do it.

Stop struggling. I was so ready to let God fix what only God could fix. Sandy had talked about letting Jesus carry our burdens, and I longed for the peace that is at the heart of genuine faith.

There were no miracles waiting when I got home and unloaded my eggs and butter and milk. I didn't go to bed that night and fall into a restful, uninterrupted sleep. I didn't wake up the next morning with a carefree heart. Some days I did struggle again and again.

But as time went on, I started sleeping better. I was able to wake up and feel hope as my companion throughout most days.

Don't misunderstand. My circumstances didn't change. Some problems took a long time to resolve, and some we're still enduring. My parents are gone, but now I look forward to being with them in heaven. The only thing that really changed was my attitude.

When I read Paul's words about learning to be content in any circumstance, I understood that true contentment would come only from knowing Jesus. I ran across some lines in Psalm 88 that caught my eye because they reminded me of Amy and her chapter about "going to ground": "I'm standing my ground, GOD, shouting for help, at my prayers every morning, on my knees each daybreak" (Ps. 88:13–18 MSG).

One afternoon I took a break from working at my computer and went outside to enjoy a day of clear spring weather. There's a creek behind my house, and I could hear it gurgling, fed by a hard rain we'd had the previous night. Early daffodils had pushed up through my flower beds, and I decided to hike down to the creek to see whether any wildflowers were popping out. I hoped that I'd find some bird feathers there and that maybe I would see some tracks left by a family of raccoons who often liked to raid my bird feeder.

But there were no feathers or tracks that day. The rain had swollen the creek until it had overflowed its banks and swept away anything that might have been there. I walked out onto a little footbridge that spanned the creek and sat down to think for a while.

It was a beautiful day. I remembered Sue Monk Kidd's story about her cocoon and how she saw it as a symbol of a new beginning for a life that had turned stale and unfulfilling.

The sun felt good on my back as it spilled through the trees, dappling the woods with shadows. Today my faith was at hand. *One day at a time,* I told myself. *God would provide when the time was right.*

After a while I decided I should get back to work, but I wanted to stay and soak up everything: the sound of the rushing water, the buds on the trees, and the warmth of the wooden bridge I was sitting on. I lay on my back for a few minutes and folded my arms behind my head as I gazed up into the canopy of trees.

Their branches were mostly bare, just beginning to show hints of pale green. I was directly underneath a beech tree, which is a kind of tree that holds on to its shriveled, brown foliage all winter long. The dead leaves don't fall until new ones unfurl in the springtime and push them off.

I was resting there, admiring the tree, when a gust of wind made the leaves sway, and I noticed something remarkable. When Sue Monk Kidd walked underneath a dogwood, she'd noticed a cocoon and took it as a sign that she needed to be strong and steady in her faith and to wait until God revealed a new path for her life.

I peered up into that towering beech tree and saw thousands and thousands of curled, furled, brown leaves dangling from every branch, a sight that startled me at first and then sent a shiver up my back. The dead leaves looked exactly like thousands and thousands of little brown cocoons, all packed with new butterflies waiting to be born, every single one of them reminding me to be patient, that God was near.

Seeds of Faith

God, thank you for the natural world, which is filled with signs of your grace and power. Help our faith grow when we encounter you in every leaf and stone. Amen.

O LORD, how many are Your works!
In wisdom You have made them all;
The earth is full of Your possessions.
                    Psalm 104:24–30 NASB

Chapter 9

A Fragile Peace

Worship the Maker of Heaven and earth, salt sea and fresh water!
—REVELATION 14:6–7 MSG

Twenty-five feet below the blue waters of the Florida straits, a statue of Jesus stands with its hands and face lifted toward the sky. The massive bronze sculpture, known as Christ of the Abyss, was a gift from Italy to America, and it's been resting on the sandy ocean floor near Key Largo Dry Rocks since 1965. For more than forty years, divers have come from all over the world to swim with schools of striped angel fish, yellowtail snappers, neon-blue gobies, skates, and spotted rays just to see this beautiful symbol of peace.

But even in such a tranquil setting, the statue hasn't always been secure. A year after its dedication at John Pennekamp State Park, a category-three hurricane named Betsy raked over the Keys, churning up the waters of the inner reef and threatening to topple the two-ton monument. With their thoughtless touching, visitors are destroying the delicate corals and sponges that make their homes around the statue's base. Fast-growing algae repeatedly form a slimy, green coat over the figure, forcing divers to scrub it clean with stiff wire brushes. Even the underwater sanctuary that encloses the sculpture suffers during the busy vacation season, when so many boaters drop anchor that the area practically turns into a marine parking lot.

Sitting on the ocean floor, lit by shafts of sunlight wavering through the crystal-clear water, the statue looks beautiful and serene—until you stop and think about all the harm that's being done by corrosive saltwater and environmental pollution, in addition to all the wear it's getting from tourists and even its cleaning crew. Then you realize that what you're seeing is really quite fragile after all. Right now, the statue is intact and appears strong, but things could change with the next violent tropical storm or reckless diver.

When things are going well, it's easy to forget that our lives are fragile too. We feel steady and secure one day, when there's a hot meal on the table and we know our children are playing nicely in the next room. Then a life-quake comes along, and everything shifts. Yesterday it was status quo; today it's all flux and change. Conflict escalates in a distant country, and our economy feels the rumble. A religious leader or politician is exposed on the nightly news, or another CEO plunders his employees' savings.

The peace we enjoyed is shattered, and suddenly, life isn't the same anymore. Faith can go overboard in times of fear and uncertainty, and you can feel yourself drowning, barely able to keep your head above water.

After our family's long season of trouble, we finally decided to take a few days of vacation. We needed the break, Bill insisted, like many people who have lived with stress for an extended period of time. We carefully watched our budget and saved enough to fund a quick trip to Florida.

Bill and Michael had talked about scuba diving for years, and because they wanted to go out on a tourist boat to try it, we marked our route on a map, loaded up the car with flip-flops and bathing suits and sunscreen, and headed south for the Keys. We'd heard that Pennekamp was an underwater paradise and the home of the famous Christ of the Abyss, also known as the Christ of the Deep. Bill wanted me to see it, as he had when he was just a boy. "It will mean a lot to you," he predicted. "You'll see. Besides, a weekend getaway will do you good."

My thoughtful husband was right. My grief over my parents, while not as raw as it had been at first, kept surfacing without warning. Spotting a woman who looked like my mother in the mall was enough to flood my eyes with tears, especially if she was accompanied by a daughter about my age. Sitting next to an older man at a school event or some other outing brought on a wave of longing for my dad. My faith was recovering, but physically and emotionally, I was tired.

When you've had to cope with too many burdens for too long, it's easy to become weak and vulnerable. Faith can become a delicate and fragile thing, as easily crushed as a seashell tumbled by the rolling waves, but I wanted my faith to keep growing and getting stronger. I wanted belief and hope to pour over me like a sweet balm, to comfort and restore and strengthen me.

C. S. Lewis once wrote that we have to learn when and how to tell our feelings to "get off" because feelings are changeable and unreliable. Negative moods can confuse and distract us from what we know to be true. That's why I love the late Oxford scholar's definition of *faith* as the art of hanging on to what our rational minds have accepted in spite of emotions that can change as fast as the weather.

As we approached Key Largo under a bright and cloudless sky, I turned my attention to the horizon and shaded my eyes to watch the sun dip into the bay, which seemed to extinguish its fiery light. The sky was the color of mangos, and my heart skipped to see its beauty.

We found a motel room for the night, and early the next morning, after a quick breakfast, we booked tickets on a charter boat that ferried passengers offshore to the watery borders of Pennekamp State Park. As we climbed aboard, other divers joined us, tossing their gear into the hold and stowing away coolers and towels, until the captain cranked the engine and cast off.

We found seats at the back of the boat, sandwiched between some life vests and water jugs, as the wind picked up and threw choppy waves at us. Not to worry, the captain said reassuringly, his voice booming over the roar of the motor. It would be a fair-weather day, and once we anchored, he'd give the divers an hour to explore the corals and tropical fish that lived below in the swaying sea grass.

"You'll see the Christ statue out there," he announced as the scuba divers began assembling their equipment, "but don't touch it. It's covered with fire coral that can sting and blister your skin."

We dropped anchor in thirty feet of clear water, and while Bill and Michael pulled on their borrowed wet suits and flippers, a crew member loaned me the gear I'd need to snorkel. Their heavy air tanks strapped on securely, the divers onboard our boat lowered their masks over their eyes; bit into their mouthpieces; and, one by one, stood on a platform behind the boat to splash into the sea.

I watched as Bill and Michael hit the water and disappeared into a vortex of bubbles, holding my breath until I saw them bob back up and signal for me to join them. With everybody off deck now except for me, I wrestled a pair of too-small fins onto my feet as the captain looked on. I tried not to let him see my sudden alarm. I'd snorkeled before, and I was an average swimmer, but I'd never been in such deep water, and my left arm was still weak from my accident. Actually, I was a little worried about whether I could handle myself in the ocean. Even climbing up and down the bobbing ladder into the water looked like a tricky proposition with only one strong hand. I glanced over the side of the boat to see whether Bill and Michael were still treading water nearby and hoped they'd remember their solemn promise to stay close by in case I had any difficulty.

"You'd better take this," the captain said, as if he'd read my mind. He tossed me a bright yellow inflatable vest. "It's made just for snorkeling. It'll let you float so you can relax while you look around."

The contraption looked embarrassingly like the water wings children wear in kiddie pools, but I didn't argue as I slipped it over my head and tightened the straps.

"Be careful out there," the captain added. He squinted into the blazing sunlight. "This is a state park, you know, and all kinds of wildlife live in parks. Humans aren't in their natural element here. You might see some barracudas, but they don't bother people during the daytime." He grinned. "They only bite after dark."

Great, I thought, as visions of sharks and eels and menacing jellyfish flashed through my mind. If I could have turned back, I would have, but all the other tourists had disappeared from sight along with, I realized, my own family. I swallowed hard, gripped the ladder with both hands, and awkwardly climbed down to ease into the sea.

Immediately a wave broke over my head, making me cough and sputter, but the water was just as inviting as I'd hoped it would be, warm from the long, sunlit days and as clear and blue as sapphire glass.

I tugged on my mask and lowered my face into the water. I could see all the way to the bottom, and I was momentarily startled to hear the raspy sound of my own breath. Floating this far out in the ocean was new to me, and now I was grateful for the yellow vest that let me lie prone in the water. All I had to do was pay attention to the current, so I wouldn't be swept too far from the boat, and occasionally flutter my fins to change direction. I willed myself to relax. *It's OK,* I told myself. *Bill and Michael have to be nearby.*

Except they weren't. I paddled and kicked and made a slow circle to look around. All I could see was the barnacled hull of the boat. All the other divers were out of sight too. *Where did everybody go?* I wondered.

With their diving gear, the others had ventured much farther from the boat and much deeper than I was able to go with just a snorkel. With a jolt I spotted a spiny creature scuttling along on the sand below me. A lobster probably, but he would have dangerous pincers. I couldn't tell exactly what he was, and I decided not to find out.

I paddled around, searching for the Christ statue, until I saw a flash of something silver and torpedo shaped hanging in the water in front of me. I stopped. The fish slowly swung around, and my heart jumped when he opened a mouthful of needle-sharp teeth. A barracuda. I stayed still until he drifted away.

I almost headed back for the ladder, wondering whether I could pull myself onboard without some help, but I didn't. We'd come such a long way, and I was longing to see that statue, just as I was longing to see God in my life. I swam around, but the ocean looked empty. All I'd seen so far were things that might be dangerous, like the spiny lobster and the barracuda. The divers had scattered, and my own family was either far away or diving deep, probably happily following some intriguing little fish or crab. I felt quite alone.

Forget it, I decided, suddenly irritated. Forget this pointless searching for things that I couldn't find no matter how hard I tried. I'd had enough, and I wanted to get back in the boat. Except now the waves were rocking it, and I had to circle around to the other side to grab the ladder. When I did, I finally saw what I had come to see.

Twenty-odd feet below me, resting on the coral reef, the magnificent Christ of the Deep statue stood with its arms raised. Jesus' gentle face was gazing up at me.

I treaded water to stay above the statue, struck by its peaceful beauty, as a stingray and a pair of angelfish swam below me. Now I understood the captain's warning about the fire corals; it was tempting to want to swim down and touch those outstretched hands. Who doesn't long to come face-to-face with the Savior?

There is a story in the Bible about a woman who had bled for many years until she saw Jesus passing by. Unable to resist, she reached out and grasped the hem of his robe, and as soon as she did, she was healed. One touch and her suffering was over.

I knew the sculpture was just a piece of stone and nothing more, and I don't believe in idols. But it did make me stop to think that I could reach out anytime to the living, risen Jesus.

Where can I go that your spirit isn't with me? asked the psalmist. "If I take the wings of the dawn, if I dwell in the remotest part of the sea, even there Your hand will lead me, and Your right hand will lay hold of me" (Ps. 139:9–10 NASB). Wherever we find ourselves, "God is a safe place to be" (Ps. 62:7–8 MSG).

Science asks for proof, for evidence that eyes can see and hands can hold; but in my experience, God doesn't work that way. Faith, as Paul pointed out, is about what we cannot see, and I was going to have to be content with that. Even more, I wanted to learn to love the mystery, to embrace it without fear or doubt or cynicism.

I spent a long time looking at the statue, and then, realizing the other divers were starting to return, I swam back toward the boat and pulled myself aboard. "How was it out there?" the captain asked, extending me a hand. He tilted his head and eyed me. "You looked kinda scared at first."

"I was for a while," I admitted. "But it was good. It was worth it."

The captain was right. The sea is not our home, and it can be filled with peril. The world isn't our real home, either, and it's frightening to think we're all alone in it.

I sat on the deck to towel the saltwater out of my hair and wait for Bill and Michael to come back in. The statue, with its open arms, had moved me, just as Bill had predicted it would. I hadn't lost my faith all at once, and it wasn't going to suddenly flood back. But I wanted it to be strong and healthy. I wanted Jesus to stay near me, in the deeps, in the valleys, anywhere the rest of my life took me. I wanted the peace that only he can give.

Once, Jesus told followers about a son who went astray. When the wandering boy returned at last, his father greeted him with great joy, sweeping him into his widespread arms. It comforts me to know that our heavenly Father also welcomes us when we come home and forgives us for our fragilities and weaknesses.

I would go on struggling and stumbling for a while longer, but Jesus was going to bring me home too. No matter how many times I got lost, he always came to find me.

I was tired after being in that rough sea for so long. As I sat waiting for the captain to pull up anchor, I leaned against the side of the boat to rest. Sunlight glimmered on the water all around me, and I tilted my head back and closed my eyes. I didn't have to see the sky to feel the warmth pouring down on me. *I must remember,* I thought, *to keep lifting my face to the Son.*

Seeds of Faith

Lord, thank you for always being near, even if I don't see you or feel you. Help me know that even when my faith is weak and frail, you are strong. Amen.

But me he caught—reached all the way
    from sky to sea; he pulled me out
Of that ocean of hate, that enemy chaos,
    the void in which I was drowning.
They hit me when I was down,
    but GOD stuck by me.
He stood me up on a wide-open field;
    I stood there saved—surprised to be loved!
                         Psalm 18:16–19 MSG

Chapter 10

Nothing without Joy

I'm singing joyful praise to God.
I'm turning cartwheels of joy to my Savior God.
—HABAKKUK 3:17–19 MSG

Each afternoon, the teachers at the Diana School in Reggio Emilia, a small town in northern Italy, put their tiny students down for their naps. But the Diana isn't any ordinary preschool, and these babies don't sleep in ordinary cribs. Here, they're tucked into soft "nests" of blankets placed on the floor so that when they wake up they don't have to wait for a caretaker to notice. As soon as their eyes flutter open, they can crawl out of their soft bundles right into the room to start exploring.

Babies on the loose? What might sound like a recipe for disaster at any other preschool is just one of the creative approaches to learning at the Diana, once named as one of the "Ten Best Schools in the World" by *Newsweek* magazine.[1] While the babies scoot across the floor to find a rattle or chase a playmate—always under the watchful eyes of their teachers, of course—the three-, four-, and five-year-olds at this innovative school might pick a few fresh leaves to glue onto their drawings of trees or take turns tumbling on rubbery gym mats piled in a corner. When they get thirsty, the children skip through the airy, light-filled rooms to the kitchen for cups of juice, and they're welcome to stay and help the cook make sandwiches for lunch.

Sixty-odd years ago, a school like this was literally a dream. After World War II, the village of Reggio was nearly reduced to rubble, its homes and businesses left shattered by bombs. But the mothers of Reggio had a dream for their children, as mothers always do. They convinced a group of parents to work together to salvage bricks from the ruined buildings and haul sand from a nearby river to construct a new school. When the school was completed in 1946, the parents invited a young teacher named Loris Malaguzzi to ride over on his bicycle. Malaguzzi liked what he saw and quickly signed on. Years later, he became the school's director and helped pioneer its unique and wonderful philosophy of learning. Today, schools like the Diana teach by encouraging children to joyfully explore the world around them—from making shadows on the floor with flashlights and paper figures to kneading dough that will make the bread for tomorrow's toast.[2] The Reggio approach has been so successful, it has become an international model for schools, studied and praised by even the prestigious Harvard Graduate School of Education. "*Niente senza gioia*," Senor Malaguzzi was fond of saying, and today his motto is painted over the doors of the school so everyone will remember: "Nothing without joy."[3] It's not only a good way to learn but a good way to live, and it's at the heart of why God sent us Jesus.

We know how to celebrate earthly things. When a baby's born, her parents send out birth announcements to share the happy news. Friends drop by with gifts and bouquets of balloons and covered casseroles, and there's a festive feeling in the air—at least until the reality of diapers and midnight feedings settles in.

When Jesus was born, God also sent out an announcement and had it delivered by an angel to shepherds tending their sheep in a starlit field. "Fear not," the angel declared, "for, behold, I bring you good tidings of great joy" (Luke 2:10 KJV). No balloons, no casseroles. But this wasn't an occasion for joy—it was a time for *great* joy because this wasn't just any baby whose birthday the world was going to celebrate. This baby had come to be our Savior. Talk about good news!

As Jesus grew up and began his earthly ministry, he taught his followers how to live blessed, happy lives. Your heavenly Father loves you, Jesus preached, and I love you also. Keep my commandments so you'll stay firmly rooted in my love. As long as you do this, your lives will spill over with gladness. "Yes, your joy will overflow!" (John 15:11 NLT). Jesus came, the Scriptures say, so that we can "enjoy life, and have it in abundance" (John 10:10 AMP).

These are wonderful, life-changing promises, but when you look around, it's tempting to wonder how they could possibly be true. Sure, it's easy for the carefree babies of Reggio Emilia to wake up every morning and toddle off on happy adventures, but what about when they grow up? What about the rest of us? Life isn't that simple.

To be human means to suffer. Sooner or later we'll grieve at a loved one's grave. We may find ourselves pulling our hair over a surly teenager or a demanding boss. Some of us will have to bury a beloved pet or make the decision to commit an incapacitated parent to long-term care. Most of us will know the sting of being passed over for a promotion, left out of a group, or forgotten on our birthday. We've felt the pain of gossip or the shame of lies and betrayals. No, life isn't always joyful. Sometimes it's almost unbearable.

But "this is the day the LORD has made," says the psalmist; "let us rejoice and be glad in it" (Ps. 118:24 NIV). Sounds crazy, doesn't it? We're supposed to be glad on every day God has made, including today? The day our plane sits on the tarmac for hours? The day the rent check bounces? When our backs ache, gas prices soar, and our first grader comes home with chicken pox or head lice?

That's right, the Scriptures insist. "Rejoice always" (1 Thess. 5:16 NASB). At first, it sounds like the Bible was written by a bunch of madmen. Who can keep a commandment like that? It's hard to imagine how life, with all its responsibilities and disappointments, could possibly be joy filled. That is, it's hard unless you know Jesus.

A lot of things can steal happiness if we're talking about a here-today-and-gone-tomorrow feeling, nothing more than the fleeting satisfaction that comes from eating a delicious meal or watching a funny movie. The Bible is talking about something else and something better. Jesus meant he had come to give us the joy of heaven, the real-deal stuff that runs deeper and lasts forever, and that's what the psalmists are telling us to celebrate. They didn't want us to forget for even a day that what is waiting for us is infinitely better than what we have right now.

Paul knew what real joy was. The apostle who endured shipwrecks and beatings also had a lifelong struggle with what he called a "thorn in the flesh" (2 Cor. 12:7 KJV). As a witness for Christ, he was scorned, arrested, and put to death. Still, he knew he was serving God, and nothing could happen to him without the Father's permission. God had a plan for Paul's life, and Paul drew peace and hope from that.

That's why people who have Jesus can go forward even when their X-rays come back marked with shadows or when they struggle with loneliness or disability. Their faith has flowered into a peace that transforms hearts and spirits. The joy of knowing Jesus grows into the hope of heaven.

That's how Joni Eareckson Tada, a quadriplegic who's been in a wheelchair since a diving accident more than thirty years ago, can travel around the world sharing the gospel with enthusiasm. That's why a half dozen silver-haired gentlemen in a retirement village roll their wheelchairs together on Sunday mornings to lift their voices and sing about God's grace and mercy.

Life isn't always good, and certainly it isn't always easy. Author and pastor Rick Warren, writing in *The Purpose-Driven Life: What on Earth Am I Here For?*, points out that it's a mistake to think God is a genie who pops out of his bottle to whip up a new car or give us a clean bill of health just because we ask.[4] There are missionaries whose congregations have covered them in prayer, yet these same men and women have been killed in other countries while doing nothing more than telling nonbelievers about Jesus. Husbands and wives have prayed for nonbelieving spouses, only to see them come to the end of their lives with their stubborn disbelief still intact. Faith has to bulk up its muscles when it stares tragedy and sorrow in the face.

So how do we hold on to hope and joy? Paul told the early church, "He is the blessed and only Ruler, the King of all kings and the Lord of all lords" (1 Tim. 6:15 NCV). The truth is that God allows everything to happen as part of a master plan, and his timing is always sound. No matter what happens to our earthly bodies, we can trust him because "we know that in all things God works for the good of those who love him, who have been called according to his purpose" (Rom. 8:28 NIV).

The prophet Isaiah compared peace to a river, but the joy of Jesus is like a river too. If you've ever taken a rafting trip, you know that feeling of being swept along by something more powerful than you are. It's exhilarating to step into the rushing water and feel yourself pulled downstream, even though realizing you're not in control can be a little scary at first.

We took our first-ever raft ride one cool spring morning when we joined a bunch of 4-H kids on a bus trip to the north-Georgia mountains. I was a little apprehensive about floating down the Chattahoochee River because I'd never done it before. I could handle an inner tube in somebody's swimming pool, but a trip in churning water? I wasn't sure I was up for it.

The kids from the 4-H club were definitely up to it. When we arrived and the driver opened the doors, they jumped over one another to get out of the bus, grabbing for the bright pink inner tubes the rafting company had provided. Some of the kids tossed their tubes into the water and jumped right in, belly first, to sail away. Michael and Bill pulled tubes over their heads like giant lifesavers and waded in while I sat down gingerly in mine.

I gasped when I hit the water; it was like plunging into a bucket of ice cubes. Everybody else was quickly sliding away downstream, so I pushed off too. The water was surprisingly fast, but of course there was no way to steer. We literally had to go with the flow.

Beside me, a kid in cutoff jeans and a T-shirt lost her grip on her tube and fell in. The river sucked the tube beyond her reach, and she started to cry until Bill tossed his tube to her. "I'll catch a ride and meet you at the pickup area," he yelled as he climbed out onto the banks. In a moment, Michael and I were pulled away too.

What have we gotten into? I thought as we bobbed and dipped and bumped into each other, trying to grip our floats and hang onto each other's foot or arm so we could stay together. For the next two and a half hours, we rode the swift water, careening from one river rock to the next, like balls bumping against the posts in a pinball game. Occasionally we hit low spots and had to hop out and launch our floats again. Other rafters kept running into us, helplessly pushed by the current, and sometimes we ran into them. When a jolt turned us over, we were dumped into pools of numbingly cold water until we could right ourselves and take off again into the sunshine.

Soaked and dunked, we grew chilled every time we drifted under the shady trees that hung over the river. *This has turned out to be a surprisingly rough ride,* I thought as I paddled hard to avoid a half-submerged branch. I wound up snagged on a hidden sandbar, stubbing my toes and making them bleed.

Shoved downriver and out of control, dumped and scratched and shivering—it sounds like we were miserable, but amazingly, we weren't. The sky overhead was the same bright blue as the morning glories that tangled over my porch back home, and the sun was high and bright. The air warmed up as the day progressed, and we caught the spicy scent of pine trees. Even through my water-spattered glasses, I could make out clumps of enormous, white-flowered rhododendrons practically beaming from the dark woods along the banks. As the river winked and sparkled in the sun and the kids in their neon-pink tubes kept laughing and trying to turn one another over, I relaxed and had fun too. So what if we weren't immune to being bumped or bruised? The rafting company that had planned our day knew this was a safe adventure. They had plenty of bandages and first-aid cream on hand for scraped fingers and toes. We didn't even mind falling off now and then. We could climb back on. The ride was so exhilarating that I felt, strangely enough, like singing.

I hadn't really wanted to come; riding for half a day on a hot bus packed with noisy kids was not my idea of a perfect day. But by the time we reached our stopping point on the river and dragged our tired bodies onto the dock, I was ready to do it again. My toes were sore, and my lips were blue from the cold, but we'd had a great time. Our day had been downright—well, joyful. For somebody like me, who usually wants to hold on tight and stay in control of everything that happens, it was a lesson in learning to let go and finding real joy in the journey, even if it was a bumpy ride.

The love Jesus pours out on the world is a lot like the river we rafted. His marvelous grace has been flowing since long before we showed up and stepped in, and it's going to keep flowing forever. The water is inviting. All we have to do is trust him to carry us along.

Rivers aren't always smooth and calm. There's always the danger that you'll hit a rough patch and wind up tossed or turned around. You may get bruised and hurt; you may travel for a time in shadows, where the darkness and the cold threaten to swallow you up. But Jesus just keeps taking you forward and buoying you up. Paul told us, "For I am convinced that neither death, nor life, nor angels, nor principalities, nor things present, nor things to come, nor powers, nor height, nor depth, nor any other created thing, will be able to separate us from the love of God, which is in Christ Jesus our Lord" (Rom. 8:38–39 NASB). Paul knew what he was talking about. He endured persecution and still was able to say, "I'm glad in God, far happier than you would ever guess." He was happy with "little as with much," with his "hands full or hands empty," thanks to "the One who makes me who I am" (Phil. 4:10–14 MSG).

When you launch out into a rushing river, you can only hope you'll be able to hang on long enough to reach your destination. Stay in God's love, and you can be sure you'll get there safely.

If we want to see heaven, Jesus taught, we have to have a child's heart. It pleases him when we come to him with outstretched hands and open minds, innocent and trusting, ready to receive his endless, boundless grace.

When the children of Reggio Emilia learn to tie their shoes, they giggle as they practice looping the laces over and over again. When they learn to count from one to ten, they recite their numbers with enthusiasm. Their teachers nod and say, Yes, that's right. *Niente senza gioia*. Nothing without joy! When we follow the Master, we're doing what children do. We're living with the joy of Jesus.

Seeds of Faith

God, thank you for the gift of your Son. We rejoice every day because our faith gives us hope and peace. Amen.

———

God himself is right alongside to keep you steady and on track until things are all wrapped up by Jesus. God, who got you started in this spiritual adventure, shares with us the life of his Son and our Master Jesus. He will never give up on you. Never forget that.

1 Corinthians 1:7–9 MSG

Chapter 11

Touchstones

On Christ the solid rock I stand,
all other ground is sinking sand.
—COMPOSER EDWARD MOTE (1797–1874)
"THE SOLID ROCK"

It might sound strange, but I keep a lot of rocks in my house. I tend to pick them up wherever I go, drawn to their rough beauty or odd shapes. I'm using a nugget of fool's gold, fished out of a creek, to hold down this month's water bill. A piece of gray granite with salt-and-pepper speckles sits on top of my computer for decoration, and I keep a deep purple amethyst crystal, a piece I bought at a hobby shop, on the fireplace mantle. On my office windowsill, I've propped up a chunk of translucent quartz, hoping it will catch the sun when it pops out from behind the clouds. Once I found a smooth, creamy-yellow stone that had a nice feel and heft; now it sits on a corner of my desk so I have something to play with when I'm talking on the phone.

I don't know what the yellow stone is. In fact, I don't even know whether a geologist would say that my finds are rocks or minerals. I can't always match them up to the postage-sized pictures in the field guide on my bookshelf, but it doesn't really matter. I enjoy looking at them and remembering where they came from, like the rose-colored rock I found on a visit to see my friend Mary in Seattle on a wintry day when snow spackled the dark fir trees in her yard. A slab of sandstone helps me recall a long-ago vacation when we drove through a spectacular canyon in Arizona.

When Michael was little, he noticed that I liked to collect interesting rocks. Sometimes I'd pick him up from preschool and find a handful of pebbles or a few flakes of shiny mica in his jacket pockets. They were gifts for me, smuggled off the playground and out from under the watchful eyes of the teacher, who didn't want her charges stowing anything they could throw at one another later, in case tempers turned cranky before naptime.

Then one day, I realized that my pocketbook felt different, a little heavier than usual. It was a couple of weeks before I stopped long enough to dig around inside and clean it out. Underneath some crumpled grocery-store coupons, a hairbrush, and my checkbook and keys, I found a layer of rocks at the bottom of my purse. Nice rocks, about the size and shape of tiny hens' eggs. I could certainly see their appeal—but they were more playground contraband, just the same.

You'd think I would have noticed the extra weight a lot sooner, but I didn't. Apparently, Michael dug them up in a playmate's yard and decided to take them home; but rather than ask me to carry his stash, he just dumped them into my bag, probably because everything else ended up in there anyway. Then he forgot his find, and I didn't even notice it.

That's how some burdens are. When you start out strong and rested, you can bear whatever you're given without a lot of effort. But as time goes by, even if your burdens don't actually become heavier, they *feel* heavier. It's not because the load has changed but because we have changed. Our energy runs out. We get tired.

Jen got tired soon after she took in her elderly, widowed mom, who had been diagnosed with Alzheimer's. Jen was glad to take her mother in, and they had a good relationship, but this aging parent refused to go gently into the good night that poet Dylan Thomas wrote about. Jen's mom cursed when she got frustrated, and she was frustrated by anything, from a jelly jar that wouldn't open to a special news bulletin that interrupted her favorite afternoon game show.

Jen tried to help. She took her mother along when she bought her groceries each week, hoping her mom would enjoy the outing. But then Jen started finding odd things in her mother's room, like one raw egg or a bar of soap—eggs that weren't missing from Jen's refrigerator and a brand of soap that the family never used. Turns out that her mom, in her deepening confusion—the same woman who once led a Girl Scout troop and sang in the church choir—had started shoplifting. Eventually, Jen's mother refused to shower or change her clothes, and she didn't want her hair brushed anymore. Before long, even close friends were finding reasons not to stop by and visit. The slow deterioration was a heavy burden for everyone who knew Jen's mom.

A few years ago, our community had to shoulder a burden that's all too familiar across the country. A boy from our high school was driving home late one rainy night when he overshot a curve on the highway. He wasn't speeding or doing anything wrong; he was just inexperienced. He hydroplaned on the water in the road, and his truck flipped over. Sadly, he'd forgotten to buckle his seat belt that evening, and he was ejected and killed. His parents spoke at the school's honors night that spring to announce a scholarship they'd established in his name. He was a great kid, his mother said, who simply made one mistake, and she wanted his classmates to remember him. After the ceremonies, his parents walked off the stage together, their heads bowed low in grief. Their pain was heavy, and I'm sure everyone who sat in the audience that night felt it too.

When my mother began her chemotherapy treatments, she faced the nausea and hair loss with her typical grace and courage, even though the doctor and nurses told us they had no cure at the time for her rare form of lymphoma. But she trusted her doctors, and she trusted God. One morning I drove over to see her, and she took off her scarf to show me her bald head. It was shocking to see at first because she'd always taken such great care with her thick, dark hair. I swallowed hard to keep from crying before I told her she was beautiful anyway, and I meant it.

She wanted me to go with her to pick out a wig, so we drove off to shop and drink coffee, as if choosing just the right hair color or style really mattered. All the time, I knew I was going to lose her, and I knew it would be soon. We found a pretty auburn hairpiece that she loved, a brighter, redder shade than her real color, and I encouraged her to buy it. She had such a flair for dressing up, and her makeup and hair, clothes and jewelry were always perfect. Somehow she understood what she was up against, but she was as OK with it as anyone could be because she had handed over her burden to a God big enough to carry it.

"Cast your cares," my wise friend Mel likes to say when I start muttering about some problem or worry. "Cast your cares." She's quoting 1 Peter 5:7. In the Amplified Bible, Peter's words are translated, "Casting the whole of your care [all your anxieties, all your worries, all your concerns, once and for all] on Him, for He cares for you affectionately and cares about you watchfully." Sometimes I take the lines apart so I can see what they really mean:

- Cast the *whole* of your care on him—everything. We're not to hold anything back.
- Cast your care *once and for all* on him. After we've given him our troubles, we shouldn't try to pick them up again.

- He cares *affectionately.* He loves us deeply, the way a father loves his little child.
- He cares *watchfully.* He keeps his eye on us, and he'll see us through whatever we have to face.

God loves us so much, he sent his Son to help us when we're weighted down with trouble. Jesus asks, in Matthew 11:28–30 (MSG), "Are you tired? Worn out? Burned out on religion? Come to me. Get away with me and you'll recover your life. I'll show you how to take a real rest. Walk with me and work with me—watch how I do it. Learn the unforced rhythms of grace. I won't lay anything heavy or ill-fitting on you. Keep company with me and you'll learn to live freely and lightly."

Most of us were brought up to think that we're supposed to be strong enough to keep pulling under any yoke, like some beast of burden, but Jesus tells us it's not about how strong we are. It's about how strong he is.

I love the story told in 1 Kings 19:5–11. That's the account of how the prophet Elijah—worn-out, discouraged, and exhausted—sat down under a broom tree in the wilderness. He had had enough; he was ready to die.

"O Lord, take my life," he cried in his despair, and then he fell asleep (1 Kings 19:4 NASB). But God is merciful, even when we cry out from the darkest places of our hearts. Unwilling to see Elijah give up, God sent an angel to minister to him.

The angel had to reach out his hand to touch Elijah, or perhaps even shake him, because the prophet was fast asleep.

But he had to get up. The angel knew his situation was bleak, and he needed help fast.

"Get up and eat," the angel commanded, and Elijah rubbed his eyes and looked around to find a cake of baked bread and a jar of water sitting nearby.

Maybe Elijah, in his brokenness, didn't have much appetite, but the angel insisted, so he ate. Then he lay down again, and the angel had to come back and repeat his urgent message. Look, the angel said, I'm serious about this. You must get up and eat some more because you're going on a journey, and it's going to be too hard if you don't take care of yourself. Elijah sat up again and took more of the bread and water, and this time he felt his stamina and strength come flooding back.

I had trouble eating after my mother died, when nothing had much taste anymore. After her funeral, I found myself almost too exhausted to function. My journey had proved too much for me, too, and my burdens were heavy. I was ready to sit down under my own tree and give up.

Then one morning Bill called me to the breakfast table. He'd made buttered toast, something my mother used to make when I stayed home sick from school. I wasn't hungry, I insisted, but he insisted back. I had to have at least a nibble.

I took a bite, and the soft bread melted in my mouth. It tasted so good because I was hungry after all. I just hadn't realized it. But it wasn't only physical hunger that was being fed. There was something restorative about the simple act of being nourished by someone who loved me. Jesus also refreshes and restores us out of his endless, boundless love. He tells us that he is the Bread of Life, able to fill us when we're hungry and satisfy us when we're thirsty: "Every person the Father gives me eventually comes running to me. And once that person is with me, I hold on and don't let go" (John 6:35–38 MSG). He has so much to offer: "My father is right now offering you bread from heaven, the real bread. The Bread of God came down out of heaven and is giving life to the world" (John 6:32–33 MSG).

Healing after my mother's death, and later after my father's, came slowly for me. I had to open my heart and spirit to receive the small, often overlooked gifts God sprinkles into our lives on a daily basis: the plate of buttered toast, a phone call from a friend with a sympathetic ear, even the surprise of seeing my mother's crimson-colored flowers sprout from seeds that had fallen in her yard to bloom again in spring. Elijah ate his cake and drank his water. He slept, ate again, and continued his journey. I've been fed, too, by a constant stream of simple blessings as I learn to walk in those "unforced rhythms of grace."

From time to time, I found myself trying to shoulder all those old burdens again. Instead of sleeping, I tossed and turned at night as my mind raced with worries about things I couldn't change, or as I grieved once again for my parents, although my faith assured me that I would see them again and that they were safe with God. When those restless nights came, I made myself stop and count the blessings of simply being alive. Even little things that might seem insignificant in the world's eyes were witnessing to me about Jesus' gentle love and care: our pets; a stranger's friendly greeting; a crisp, green apple to eat; or a second chance at anything.

If you're tempted to hang on to your burdens, too, turn to chapters 3 and 4 in the book of Joshua and read how God instructed Joshua to have the priests carry the ark of the covenant over the Jordan River. This would have happened during the harvest season, when the Jordan was high enough to flood its banks. Yet the moment the priests' feet touched the water, the river stopped flowing.

The men were startled, but they did as God commanded and started walking across the now-dry riverbed. At the halfway point, they stood with the ark balanced between them until the entire nation of Israelites crossed to the other side. Next, God told Joshua to pick twelve men, one from each tribe, and have them gather stones from the riverbed. They were to stack the stones where they planned to camp for the night. The place where the stones were laid became known as Gilgal, which means a circle of stones or an altar.

Finally, the priests walked the rest of the way over the Jordan and delivered the ark to the other shore. Once everyone was safe, God allowed the waters of the Jordan to rush together again.

Joshua knew that one day the Israelites' descendants would see the twelve stones at Gilgal and ask their ancestors, "What do these stones mean?" (Josh. 4:21 NIV). The stones, he would tell them, were there to serve as a reminder of what God had done for them. The rocks were meant to be touchstones for future generations, markers that would help them see how far they'd come, not only on their physical journey but also in their spiritual lives.

When I'm in my office working, I like to handle the rocks I keep near my desk. The piece of granite, those smooth pebbles from the long-ago playground, the yellow stone—they all remind me of the trips I've taken and the places I've seen. When I look at everything that has happened in my life, I remember my spiritual journey too. Just as the people did so long ago, I can count God's many mercies, recalling not only all he can do but also how heavy things are when I try to carry them alone.

Seeds of Faith

God, thank you for the touchstones in our lives. They help us look back and remember that you have always been with us, and you always will be. Amen.

O come, let us sing for joy to the Lord,
Let us shout joyfully to the rock of our salvation.
Psalm 95:1 NASB

Chapter 12

Walking in Faith

For we walk by faith, not by sight.
—2 CORINTHIANS 5:7 KJV

Kids always get restless at the end of a school year, lured by the promise of lazy summer days ahead. By the time they're high-school seniors, however, they can barely wait to grab those diplomas and race forward into their adult lives. Michael was no exception. He started filling out college applications months before he was due to graduate, taking his counselor's advice to apply to more than one place. She recommended that each senior send his paperwork to at least two schools: one that was sure to accept him, based on his SAT scores and grades, and then to the one he really wanted to go to, a dream school. Michael's ideal school was a well-regarded research university that specialized in the field he wanted to study.

Because his heart was set on attending that big school, Bill and I wanted it for him, too, and we watched him work toward it throughout his high-school years, taking tough courses, such as advanced calculus and chemistry, and participating in extra-curricular activities that he truly enjoyed but that he'd also been told would improve his chance of acceptance.

We were happy when the "sure-thing" school really did turn out to be a sure thing, and his application was accepted right away. But as graduation got closer, we started to get worried about his dream school. That university had promised to notify all its applicants, whether they were accepted or rejected, by mid-March that year. By the end of February, we still hadn't heard a word.

I tried to stay busy, but as the days slipped by, I found myself constantly watching for the mail carrier, who drove a little postal truck with a distinctive whine. Michael made me promise that if "The Envelope" came, I would send him a text message at school or come and get him—he was that uptight. Although I initially felt pretty calm, willing to accept whatever God sent for him, I was getting more and more stressed too. His anxiety was rubbing off on me, even while I tried to tell him not to worry, that God was in control. Still, I rushed outside every time I heard the mail truck go by.

Michael predicted that we'd know what the answer was before we even ripped open the envelope. A standard-sized letter would mean a rejection. A thick manila envelope, stuffed with brochures about student housing, schedules, and financial aid, would deliver the good news.

We ripped another calendar page off the wall, and Michael's hopes rose and fell. Other kids he knew who had also applied to the dream school were beginning to get their letters, and almost all of them were positive. Some nights he got out of bed and came into our room, asking over and over whether we thought he had a good chance of getting in. Bill and I had been praying about college for a long time, but we started praying extra hard about the dream school.

Keep the faith, we told him. No matter where you go, God is taking you there. You'll have to step out in trust and leave this up to him, confident that God sees the big picture and has a perfect plan for your life.

But to be honest, after I said all these reassuring things to my son, I sneaked off to bite my nails and pace the floor. I'm not proud of this because it shows that my faith sometimes stands on pretty wobbly legs. It means that while I love God and want to trust him, I'm still stubbornly hanging on to other stuff that I really should hand over to him. It's like I've got a death grip on certain issues, and while I want to give them up—I really do—I have a hard time. I'm a lot like a kid who longs to ride the roller coaster and then finally musters up the courage to climb aboard. There are long stretches on the ride when I relax and actually enjoy myself, feeling confident that I'm safe, that I'm moving along nicely and that my destination is in sight. Then the coaster starts rattling up an especially steep hill. I look down to see how far away the ground is and how far I could fall. I get scared, thinking I'm about to plummet over the top and go racing down the other side, out of control, hair streaming out behind me and the wind taking my breath away.

When I stop to think I'm not running the train, my impulse is to hang on tighter than ever, but that's just because I forget there's a conductor at the controls, and he knows what he's doing.

In Michael's case, it wasn't that I didn't believe God could bring his dream to pass or would provide a good college. I just didn't want Michael to be disappointed about *this* dream and *this* school, and I knew that sometimes God says no or, at least, not now. I kept praying, but my prayers began to subtly shift. Instead of asking for God to send Michael where he wanted him to go, I started pleading: God, let *this* research university accept him because it's what his heart desires. Looking back, I guess I was trying to talk God into seeing things my way. Then, like a guilty afterthought, I would add: But, hey—if this isn't your will, Lord, we'll submit to your authority. Just let it be your will, OK?

Not exactly a submissive prayer, but there you have it. I wanted God to lead us. I just wanted to tell him where.

Finally, none of us could stand the waiting anymore, so Michael decided to visit the university and speak to an admissions counselor in person. He located the man's office and took his turn in a line of kids waiting to do the same thing. The counselor listened attentively as Michael recited his qualifications. Great GPA, the man said, nodding. Good test scores. Michael's application, he thought, had probably been deferred, not because he wasn't a good candidate but because he might not be quite good enough. There were many top-achieving candidates this year, and they were sorry, but they just couldn't take everybody. His admission would depend on how many people they could accept before they simply filled up all the freshmen slots.

We kept hoping, and we weren't alone. The local paper carried an article from the wire services about parents and kids facing disappointment all over the country. The story reported that Harvard was actually turning away students with perfect 800 scores on their SAT math exams. Princeton was rejecting kids with 4.0 grade point averages. The problem, the article said, was that the children of baby boomers were graduating in record numbers, overcrowding the best colleges.[1] Dreams were being dashed everywhere. We started praying harder.

Now the notification deadline got even closer. Acceptance notices kept rolling into mailboxes around town—except for ours. Eventually, Michael was the only one left waiting.

March 14 came. One more day, and we would know one way or the other, good news or bad. That morning, while I was home alone, I heard the mail truck coming down our street. My legs felt as limp as noodles, but I ran down the driveway and yanked open the mailbox door. There was an envelope, finally, with Michael's name on it.

And it was the small one.

Kids don't always understand when parents tell them we'd rather bear any hurt than see them in pain, but it's true. I wanted to go back in the house, plop down on the kitchen floor, throw a dish towel over my head, and weep. On top of everything else, I was going to have to be the bearer of the bad news.

I had all day to mourn before Michael came home from school, so I talked to God. I'm not happy, I told him, and I don't understand why this had to happen. Haven't we had enough trouble in the past few years? I felt bitter, hurt, and sad, all at once, knowing how badly this was going to go over with my boy. Like a knee-jerk reaction, my old negative attitude kicked in. God had abandoned us. God didn't care. I had to make an effort to shut down the shrill voices shrieking in my ears.

It took me a little while to settle down but not as long as it once did. I prayed, and finally I was able to say, OK, God. I promised to submit to your authority, and now I have to keep my word. I don't want to, but I will. I don't know why your answer was no, but if it was important for me to understand, you'd make it clear. Meanwhile, you're God, and I'm not. I may not like it, but I'm going to trust you on this because I know you love me, and you love Michael. Your Word says you have a purpose for us. You've said you will direct our paths and guide our lives, and you never go back on a promise.

I also asked God to help me find a way to talk to Michael and help him through this. Hours later, he came home from school and headed for the refrigerator, as was his habit. He opened the door and took out the milk jug, unscrewed the top, and swallowed a big glug.

I dreaded what I had to say. "The school's decision came today," I managed to croak, willing myself not to get weepy. "It's not the news you wanted."

He didn't say anything, just cocked his head to one side and put down the milk as he looked at me quizzically. I handed him the letter and waited with my hand on his shoulder as he read it. After a minute, he tossed it onto the counter and climbed the stairs to his room without a word.

I gave him some time before I followed. We talked a lot that afternoon; and we grieved together because people grieve when a dream dies, and it's better to grieve with someone who loves you.

Why? he asked, just as I knew he would.

His disappointment was just that: a disappointment, not a tragedy, and I don't want to make too much of it when other people have faced so much worse. Tragedies happen on a much bigger scale and often change our entire lives, but Michael was young, and he didn't know this yet. He simply didn't have enough experience to see that the end of one dream doesn't mean the end of everything. For the moment he was devastated, and he wanted an answer. Why, when we had prayed, when this meant so much, did God choose to say no?

When life runs off in a ditch, it's tempting to try to explain, but most of the time we're just reciting tired clichés. Bereaved parents have heard it before. The baby they just buried? Friends murmur sentiments that belong on greeting cards, about how heaven needed another angel. The small business-man who goes bankrupt? The ordeal will make him stronger, his relatives murmur hopefully. The cancer that comes back after we thought it was defeated? Neighbors say that burdens are given only to those strong enough to bear them. But suffering makes the questions surface again and again. Why me? Why now?

We have to be careful of trying to wave questions away when people are in pain. Easy answers can be hard to swallow. Clichés don't solve chronic problems. Pat replies don't heal deep hurt. What we can do when we're not sure why things happen is to focus on God instead of on the situation.

As Michael and I talked that afternoon, I told him about an interview the Reverend Billy Graham had given. Reportedly, the minister and his crusade team had just finished a crusade in one city when they rushed to the airport to catch a flight to the next stop on their itinerary. When they arrived, the ticket agent apologized, saying the flight had been overbooked and all the seats were taken. The team would have to wait for a later departure. Graham and the other men found a quiet place to pray and ask God to make space for them, somehow, so they could get on the plane and keep their appointment. But God said no. The plane left without them, with every seat filled—and tragically crashed before it got to its destination, killing some of the passengers. In hindsight, Rev. Billy Graham said he believed God said no to protect him, and he gave God the glory for keeping them safe.

But the reporter pressed on with his interview. What about the other people on that flight? he asked. Surely the reverend didn't think his life, or his team's, was more important than anyone else's. So why didn't God protect them too? Could he please explain this apparent contradiction?

Rev. Billy Graham didn't even try. I don't know why, he admitted in his honest, thoughtful way, because of course God loved and cared for all the people on that plane. In spite of the disaster, he added, he was absolutely certain that God was in control that day, and there was a reason for what happened. God is trustworthy and just, good and loving.

I loved his reply because it made so much sense to me. I can't understand why so much suffering goes on in the world, but I can grasp the basic truth that God cares. I can also accept that much of what happens in life is beyond my limited human ability to ever understand. I can't quote the principle of gravity; I've heard that even scientists aren't sure why a fat bumblebee has the ability to fly. So why should I expect to understand or explain God? I am content to accept the seeming paradox that a loving God could allow what seemed like a tragedy because he is trustworthy.

This was the same answer Bill and I tried to give Michael after he read his rejection notice. We didn't know why he didn't get into his dream school, when things looked so promising, although we told him we could look to the Bible for clues to God's purposes and perhaps we would understand it in the future. Maybe, we admitted, we never would.

But if we never figured out the why of this situation, we assured him it was still OK because God loves him. We also urged him to tell God how sad and disappointed he was because God longed to hear about everything in his life, and he could and would make something good out of this experience. Because of Jesus, we assured our son, he could be hopeful about tomorrow.

Peace of mind comes from knowing that God has a plan for every life. The One who gives the stars their glow, the Creator who puts the starfish in the sea and unfolds a tulip's colorful petals from a humble bulb, is faithful. He'll give you strength to do all things, we told Michael, if you'll walk with Jesus and let him lead.

When Michael was a baby, Bill and I used to watch and bite our lips as he learned to walk. We longed to hold his hands as he lurched from chair to sofa to ottoman, but we knew we had to let him go or he'd never toddle on his own. When he lost his balance and fell, we picked him up and set him on his feet again, and most of the time he grinned and took right back off. Instead of being discouraged, he seemed to think all that stumbling and tumbling were just part of some grand adventure.

Now that he had become a young man, we saw that we had a much bigger teaching job ahead of us. This time we had to teach him to walk in faith, and unless we were hypocrites, we needed to walk right alongside him in confidence and hope. We had to show him that when he couldn't see the evidence of God with his eyes, his beliefs would help him stand.

Babies are quick to master those first few physical steps, but when children get older, it's harder to learn new skills. It can take a lifetime to master a walk of faith.

As for me, I'm still practicing. I want to get it right because I want to walk with Jesus too. Bill and I also want to do what Moses told the Israelites to do when he preached to them from the plains of Moab. He commanded them to stay close to God, remembering what the Lord had done for them: "Keep close watch over yourselves. Don't forget anything of what you've seen. Don't let your heart wander off. Stay vigilant as long as you live. Teach what you've seen and heard to your children and grandchildren" (Deut. 4:9 MSG).

As I write these words, Michael is attending another school that offers the same course of study, one that will allow him to transfer into the dream university if he successfully completes the required classes. He still wishes he'd gotten in from the beginning, though, and he still very much wants to know why God said no or, at least, not now. Why do such things happen?

Unless God decides to tell us, we remind him, we can learn to live in the mystery because, as Paul said, we can only see through a dark and smoky glass right now. One day we'll see plainly. Until then, if we stumble in our doubts, we'll pick ourselves up and get going again. Like a baby trying his first steps, we could look at this phase of Michael's life as a grand adventure, led by a trustworthy and loving Lord.

"So what do you think?" Paul asks in the book of Romans. He's convinced that we can be hated or homeless, bullied or backstabbed, disappointed or downcast, but nothing—absolutely nothing at all—can separate us from God's endless mercy and grace.

"With God on our side like this, how can we lose?" (Rom. 8:31 MSG). That's the question we really need to ask. Our hope lies in knowing that whatever path we're walking, he is walking too.

Seeds of Faith

Lord, thank you for letting us ask boldly for the desires of our hearts, but help us mean it when we say we'll bow to your authority. We know you love us and you want what is best for us. Amen.

And you will make a new start, listening obediently to God, keeping all his commandments that I'm commanding you today. God, your God, will outdo himself in making things go well for you.

Deuteronomy 30:8–9 MSG

Chapter 13

Jesus Shout

Some trust in chariots, and some in horses,
but we will remember the name of the LORD our God.
—PSALM 20:7 KJV

R ecently, my friend Martha has been teaching a class of four-year-olds at our church. Most of the group are little boys, and she says they remind her of a pack of feisty bear cubs, pouncing on one another and rolling around on the floor to wrestle. Sometimes things get so lively, one of the other teachers has to jump in and untangle the tumbling ball of bodies. The constant activity makes for a pretty exciting Sunday-school lesson every week.

Lately, Martha has been teaching her kids about Jesus, telling them stories of his miracles and using Theo, the doggie sock puppet, to help them visualize how Jesus traveled around the countryside sharing God's love. At the end of storytime, when Theo slips back into his box for a rest, Martha passes out animal crackers and asks her energetic class a few questions to find out whether anything she said has actually gotten through.

Her fond hope is that at least a little bit of the Good News will sink in while all the crayon-coloring and Lego-tossing and "Stop touching me!" stuff is going on.

These kids are smart. They figured out fast that if they shout, "Jesus!" that's the right answer to almost any question Martha is going to pose. Their strategy works great when she wants to know "Who loves us?" or "Who is God's Son?" But the answer sounds a little strange when another teacher comes in to ask, "Who wants another cracker?"

"Jesus!" they yell in unison, and Martha, who's too kind to turn down anybody who might need a snack, especially Jesus, just laughs and rips open another package.

There's a lot of power in names. Mothers who sleep hard after a long day at the office and an equally long evening in the kitchen, scraping lasagna off dirty dinner plates and trying to explain why anybody would ever really use something as boring as long division, still jump out of bed the moment a toddler with an earache wails, "Mama!" Playground bullies know that cruel names can intimidate and demean. Madison Avenue is definitely savvy: advertisers recognize that the right label can persuade us to buy everything from designer shoes to luxury cars to a celebrity's brand of salad dressing.

In the Old and New Testaments, names often gave clues to a person's character or lineage; and when those names changed, it meant something important was about to happen. Abram, whose name meant "high or exalted father," was ninety-nine years old when God announced that he would make him the father of many nations, despite his advanced age. To seal their covenant, God changed his name to Abraham.

Simon was an ordinary fisherman out casting his nets for sardines, mullet, and tilapia in the beautiful blue Sea of Galilee when his name changed too. He might have been tired and hot, stinking of fish and sweat after a long day on the water, when his brother Andrew came running up to tell him that the long-awaited Messiah had finally appeared. Can you imagine how astonished Simon was when he went to meet Jesus and the Master recognized him at first glance? In effect, Jesus looked up and said, Oh, no introductions needed. I already know you. You're Simon, John's son. But starting today, I'm giving you a new name, and everybody else will call you by it too. From now on, you'll be known as Peter. Because Peter translates as "rock," the name change signaled a sea change in the simple fisherman's life. He would become the foundation for Jesus' church; he would learn how to fish for men.

The only name that never changes, and the name above all other names, is Jesus. It's the only name with perfect power to save and comfort, redeem and heal.

Just like Martha's bear-cub boys, Peter eventually figured out that Jesus' name carried a lot of weight. He saw what it could do after Jesus ministered to a crowd of five thousand followers who listened to Jesus preach and then sat down, hot and weary, to rest beside a lake. Peter carefully watched as his Lord divided five loaves of bread and two fishes into a meal that filled their empty stomachs. Later, Peter and the other disciples took a boat, as Jesus had instructed them to do, and crossed over to the other side of the lake while the crowd gathered their things and left for home.

But without Jesus, things did not go well for the men. The book of Matthew tells us that night fell soon after they pushed off from shore. "Meanwhile, the disciples were in trouble far away from land, for a strong wind had risen, and they were fighting heavy waves" (Matt. 14:24 NLT).

In trouble. Matthew doesn't tell us exactly what lake or sea they were on, but he does say that Jesus and his disciples had traveled to a remote place after hearing of the death of John the Baptist. It's OK if we can't pinpoint their precise location. We don't have to know the geography to know what Matthew meant. Trouble is a universal address, and like Peter, we've all been there.

Because these were fishermen, experienced with fast-changing weather and choppy seas, they knew they were in danger when they saw a storm brewing as the sun sank into the waves. All night long the boat rocked beneath their feet until they looked toward the horizon at dawn and rubbed their tired, red eyes in astonishment. Jesus, their Master, was walking toward them, striding over the waves.

Don't be afraid, Jesus called out, knowing how they'd panic to see a ghostly figure striding through the gloom, much less walking on water as no human could do. Peter must have strained his eyes to see because he asked, Is that you, Lord? If it is, tell me to come out there where you are.

Out into the churning water? Out into the darkness? Even though getting out of the boat would be perilous, Peter instinctively realized that anywhere with Jesus is better than anywhere without him. Suddenly he slung first one leg and then another over the side of his craft.

For a moment all was well. Peter shivered as his feet hit the cold water and the spray splashed onto his clothes. He stood up, balanced on the waves, and as long as Peter kept his eyes on the Lord, he was safe.

Then something happened. Maybe he heard the shouts of the startled men behind him as they yelled, What are you doing, you madman? Come back here before you drown! Maybe he listened to an inner voice that whispered, You can't do what you're trying to do. No human can. And how could *he* help you, anyway? In this storm, you'll have to save yourself! Peter blinked, and waves of doubt, more chilling than the water at his feet, rushed over him. Faith momentarily collapsed, and he sank into the white caps.

Just before he went under, Peter remembered that there was a name he could call on for help, a Friend who wouldn't fail him, and he uttered his own "Jesus shout."

"Lord, save me," he cried (Matt. 14:30 KJV).

What happened next is what always happens when we use that name. Jesus reached out, grabbed Peter by the arm, and pulled him to safety. "You have so little faith," Jesus said as Peter tumbled into the boat, gasping for breath. "Why did you doubt me?" (Matt. 14:31–32 NLT).

I've read that passage dozens of times, and I always wonder what tone of voice Jesus used when he said it. Did he shake his head and smile at Peter's all-too-predictable behavior? Did he cluck his tongue like a forgiving parent whose child keeps testing his boundaries? Or did Jesus speak with a sad voice and weary eyes as he chastised the friend who should have known better, who should have believed after all he had already seen and experienced?

I'm afraid Jesus was disappointed. But here's the good news: Jesus also understood. He knows that faith can ebb and flow, just like the tides that wash the shore. He knows that when we're tired or weak, frightened or storm-tossed, our faith can buckle and let us fall.

Sometimes we're like the man who brought his deaf-mute son to Jesus, pleading for help in casting out the boy's demon. Like that father, we have enough faith to come to Jesus in the first place. But there's still something lacking. I believe you can help my son, the man told Jesus, but please, help me believe even more!

Faith and doubt coexist like that for many of us, two faces of the same coin; but what is important to remember is that Jesus didn't turn the man away, even though his faith was shaky. Just as Jesus reached out and took Peter by the arm to save him, he restored the tormented boy to health. Jesus will help us believe, and believe even more, when we ask.

After Jesus ascended into heaven, Peter remembered the power in Jesus' name and used it when he spotted a crippled man begging for money at the temple gate. I know you're in need, Peter told the beggar, but I have a better gift than money for you. In Jesus' name, get up and walk. After a lifetime of lying on a mat at the feet of passersby, the man didn't just walk—he leaped up and danced, jubilant, praising God, rejoicing. The crowd looked on, hardly able to believe their eyes, and Peter was surprised by their surprise.

Don't you know, he asked them, what faith can do? It might have taken a good dunking, but Peter had finally learned the power of Jesus' name.

Sometimes we forget to call on Jesus when we're in trouble. But Jesus never forgets us, and neither does our heavenly Father.

When Michael is afraid he'll forget someone's name—or anything important, like a homework assignment—he writes a note on his own hand. Instead of reaching for a piece of notebook paper or a sticky note, he'll ink a reminder up and down his arm or in the palm of his hand. Writing on your skin probably isn't healthy, and I don't recommend it, but he insists that it is effective. He can't miss seeing "study chapter 10" or "do vocab words" when he's washing up for dinner.

Amazingly, the Scriptures use a similar image to describe how close we are to God's heart and how unforgettable we are to him. "Look," he tells us in Isaiah 49:16 (MSG), "I've written your names on the backs of my hands."

God doesn't intend to lose us, no matter what happens. A bad marriage can't separate us from the love of God, nor can a bad diagnosis. A wrong decision won't do it, or an unhealthy habit, or a negative attitude. If we wander, the Father sends the Son, Jesus, the Good Shepherd, to go out and bring us back into the fold.

Some people don't like the image in the Bible that refers to Jesus as a shepherd and to us, his followers, as sheep. Sheep, they protest, are dumb-as-rocks creatures. They bunch up in bleating, noisy flocks and let anybody lead them around. Even a dog can herd sheep, they say, so how smart can they be? It's true that sheep aren't the brightest creatures in the barnyard, so no, in that sense it's not particularly flattering to be counted among them.

But focusing on a sheep's IQ misses the point. The Bible calls us sheep because the animals are valued and loved by their masters, just as we're valued and loved.

Brenda McKaig knows how valuable sheep are.[1] Brenda is a shepherd (she doesn't care for the word *shepherdess*) who tends a woolly flock of gentle Finnsheep on her farm near the line that separates Georgia and Tennessee. Brenda and her veterinarian husband, Robert, take care of everything their sheep need.

In very early spring, after the ewes birth their lambs, Brenda gets up night after night in the cold and dark to go out into the pasture and check on them. Sometimes she has to chase off coyotes, or she rescues newborns that have gotten separated from their mothers before they perish in the freezing temperatures before dawn.

In the summertime Brenda has to catch each one of her sheep and shear it. It's a hot, dirty job to pin a big, unhappy sheep to the ground long enough to run clippers through its thick, matted wool. Later, she collects the wool, washes it, and spins it into yarn that she dips into colorful dyes. She weaves the yarn on an antique loom to make jackets and shawls or knits the skeins into hats and scarves that she sells to help support her farm. All of her handmade items are useful and beautiful reminders of her animals.

Because Brenda values her sheep, she knows them all by name, and she remembers what makes each one unique. Brownie, Nestle, and Cocoa have chocolate-black fleeces. Scarlett likes to get a nice scratch between the ears. Mischievous Gracie unties tennis shoes and pulls the strings out of jackets when Brenda takes her to visit the kids at Vacation Bible School or loans her out to area churches for their Christmas nativity scenes. Sweet Virginia, who has a gentle disposition, is Brenda's companion on road trips to county fairs.

When I stroll into Brenda's pasture, I can't tell one sheep from another aside from the color of their coats. They're all about the same size and height, and they all have very similar faces. They even behave the same way; when Brenda rattles a feed bucket, they all hurry toward the barn and jostle one another as they compete for room at the food trough.

But Brenda has raised many of these sheep from birth. She remembers the ones she had to hand feed with a baby bottle. She knows which ewe stays calm when the big clippers come out and which one goes a little goofy when it's time to be sheared. Brenda can even pick out her sheep by the sound of their deep, plaintive voices. Because she cares for them and about them, she sees each fluffy ball of wool as an individual with its own personality.

Jesus knows each of us, too, and cares for us as tenderly as any shepherd cares for a flock. He looks for us when we're lost in the dark; he rescues us when we're in trouble. He knows us intimately and invites us to know him. He delights in our voices and longs for us to talk to him in prayer. He knows us by name, just as we know his.

In the end, those feisty little boys in Martha's Sunday-school class have it exactly right. It doesn't matter what the question is. It doesn't matter what the problem is, or the doubt or the fear. Whether you shout it from the mountains or whisper it into your pillow in the dark, the answer to everything is *Jesus*.

Seeds of Faith

Lord, help me remember the power in your name. Teach me to call on you and to watch, believing, for your help to appear. Thank you for holding me close to your heart. Amen.

Jesus Shout

Thank you! Everything in me says, "Thank you!"
Angels listen as I sing my thanks.
I kneel in worship facing your holy temple
*   and say it again: "Thank you!"*
Thank you for your love,
*   thank you for your faithfulness;*
Most holy is your name,
*   most holy is your Word.*
The moment I called out, you stepped in;
*   you made my life large with strength.*
                              Psalm 138:1–3 MSG

Chapter 14

All You Really Must Know

By faith in the name of Jesus, this man whom you see
and know was made strong.
—ACTS 3:16 NIV

If you've ever driven through Atlanta, which is my hometown, you've probably been confused by all the road signs with "Peachtree" in their names. The original Peachtree Street, which runs north and south, makes up the heart of the city, and that's where you'll find most of the landmarks that we're known for: the High Museum of Art and the Atlanta Symphony Center; many prominent banks and law firms; and a luxurious old movie palace designed to look like a Moorish castle, known as the Fabulous Fox Theater.

Georgia's nickname is the Peach State, which goes a long way toward explaining why our city planners didn't stop with naming only one street in honor of our famous fruit. We also have

Peachtree Lane, Peachtree Plaza, Peachtree Hills, and Peachtree Road. There are Peachtree Valley, Circle, Court, Parkway, Trail, and Walk, as well as Peachtree Drive, Avenue, Way, and Boulevard. Then the madness starts all over with directional names like West Peachtree Street, Peachtree Place North, and so forth. Even the natives get lost here.

I've never been good at navigating Atlanta's roads, many of which are especially frustrating because they are designated one-way or exit only. Evidently, the engineers who built them never foresaw Atlanta's incredible population boom, and our streets can't handle all the cars. In fact, one high-traffic area, commonly known as Five Points, actually began as the convergence of two dirt trails used by Creek Indians on their way to a village called—you could almost guess—Standing Peachtree.

Today, Five Points refers to the intersection of two legs of Peachtree Street—the main Peachtree that runs north and south—and three other major thoroughfares. Once I got so lost in our downtown area, I thought I'd have to call Bill to come and get me—but I didn't even know how to tell him where I was. Finally, I pulled over to park, then got out and walked a couple of blocks until I spotted a landmark I could recognize. At any other crossroads, I would have had a fifty-fifty chance of making the correct turn, but I knew the odds were against me with five choices at hand.

Everyone encounters a crossroads at some time in life, when it's difficult to know exactly what lies ahead, but making the wrong decision and heading down the wrong road can have serious consequences. Do we pass up a chance to pad an expense account and take home a few extra bucks from a big corporation that probably won't miss the money anyway? Should we repay someone who has injured us with a harsh tongue-lashing or hold our tongues instead and greet our enemy with charity and forgiveness? What are we to make of God, and how do we live in faith when life turns out to be difficult or painful, demanding or discouraging?

The book of Jeremiah has a lot to say about what we should do when things get rough, and it addresses who God really is and what he expects from us. As it turns out, disasters and problems can reveal God to us in ways we'd never even thought about before.

Jeremiah, one of the best-known Old Testament prophets, had a long relationship with God, and his distress over the wrong choices his people made caused him to earn his nickname as "the weeping prophet." He certainly had reasons to weep. Jeremiah saw the tribes of Judah worshipping false prophets, and he passionately preached the need to repent before God turned his wrath on the nation. For more than twenty years, Jeremiah urged the Hebrews to turn away from their sins, but they ignored his warnings until, eventually, the Babylonians attacked and Judah fell into captivity.

Before this happened, God gave Jeremiah a message to deliver so his people could respond and get their lives back on track. "Go stand at the crossroads and look around," God directed Jeremiah to say. "Ask for directions to the old road, the tried-and-true road. Then take it. Discover the right route for your souls" (Jer. 6:16–20 MSG).

It's clear that God did not want to punish the disobedient, preferring instead to give them every chance to set things right and renew their devotion to him. Sadly, Jeremiah's hardheaded people didn't listen. They stood at the crossroads, all right, but they decided to head off in every other direction, unwilling to take the path God had planned for them.

Sooner or later, everyone has to make a choice between sticking with God or striking out on his own. Staying on the road to faith is a challenge because we'll always encounter crossroads and contradictions. Inexplicable mysteries are everywhere. Temptations and doubts and fears abound.

But we do have compasses to help us find the way. Gratitude can point us in the right direction, remembering that "the Lord's love never ends; his mercies never stop. They are new every morning" (Lam. 3:22–23a NCV). Through Jesus, our Father releases us from sin's hold, and when we accept him, we're given the gift of new and spotless hearts. We can stop worrying about our daily bread because Jesus reminds us to look at the sparrows and see how abundantly God provides for even the least of his creatures. When we see a field of daylilies lifting gold and yellow blossoms to the sun, we can rest assured that he'll give us our everyday needs, such as clothing and shelter.

Hope also leads us to the right road. Joy is the watchword for a believer's life because, as Luke wrote, there's no more death for us, and we can be sure that our loved ones are safe with God. "Brothers and sisters," Paul told the Thessalonians, "we want you to know about those Christians who have died so you will not be sad, as others who have no hope. We believe that Jesus died and that he rose again. So, because of him, God will raise with Jesus those who have died" (1 Thess. 4:13–14 NCV).

When I come to a confusing fork in the road, I look to God's love, more than any other marker, to show me the way. Several years ago, Robert Fulghum, an author, lecturer, and former minister (who lists his credits as a singing cowboy and ditchdigger, among many other talents), wrote a slender volume called *All I Really Need to Know I Learned in Kindergarten.* His collection of good-humored essays became a best seller and an instant classic for its celebration of the simple, ordinary things in life.

What does Mr. Fulghum share in his books that strikes such a deep chord with readers? He tells wonderful stories, for one thing, like the tale about a shoe repairman who, when he couldn't mend a customer's shoes, returned them with cookies tucked inside to ease any disappointment. But Robert Fulghum also tapped into some universal truths when he drew up a list of lessons from his kindergarten days. Items on the list proved to be fine guideposts for grown-up lives too—like his admonition to stop and apologize when you've hurt someone or to play fair in everything you do.

After I read his book, I realized that I'd learned everything I needed to know not in kindergarten but in Sunday school.

One of my earliest memories is singing a hymn composed around 1860, and chances are, you know it too. It's the first song most children who go to Bible school are taught to sing: "Jesus loves me! This I know, for the Bible tells me so; little ones to Him belong; they are weak, but He is strong."[1]

Jesus loves me. That's the most important lesson I heard in Sunday school, and if I had to pare down all I ever learned into just one key point, that's the one I'd pick. In his Gospel, John tells us what love is truly all about: it's not our affection for God but the marvelous, perfect love God showed to the world when he sent his Son to blot out our sins.

How do we thank the Father for such a gift? Paul tells us to go out and live a life that overflows with love, the kind that spills over onto other people. We can strive to be like Christ, who "gave himself for us as a sweet-smelling offering and sacrifice to God" (Eph. 5:2 NCV). At my church, the pastor raises his arms over the congregation at the end of each worship service and gives the benediction "Friends, believe the Good News." I love hearing that, because God's grace poured out to the world through the gift of his only Son is good news indeed, and I want to share it.

God loves us, forever and always. That's what we need to know when we bump up against financial burdens, disabilities, job loss, or even death. God will never stop loving us, and that's what we should hang on to when we're lonely or tempted, sad or depressed, addicted or grieving. His mercy saves us, and it can save a hurting world if only we'll pass it along. "He is the

Father of mercies," the Scriptures say, "and the God of all comfort" (2 Cor. 1:3 HCSB).

Years ago I sat in a doctor's office complaining of my inability to get a good night's sleep. Too many cares weighed on me and too much grief, and I found myself winding my bedcovers into a snarl every evening as I tossed and turned with insomnia. "I think I'm falling apart," I told my physician. "My life is a train wreck."

She looked up at me without missing a beat. "You're not falling apart," she said firmly. "You're still here, aren't you?"

I am still here—not the same person I once was, perhaps, but that's OK. I'd rather be tried and tested and know Jesus than to have sailed through life and never reached out to find him.

Another woman, a long time ago, reached out to Jesus, too, and we have her story in the book of Matthew. We don't know exactly what her problem was, except that she'd been suffering from some sort of hemorrhage for more than a decade—a lifetime for someone who might have had children who needed her, a husband who loved her, a house that needed cleaning, or meals that had to be prepared.

Apparently, the woman had been hearing about Jesus and his marvelous works, and when he came to visit her village, she fell in with the crowds that were following him. "Just then, a woman who had suffered from bleeding for 12 years approached from behind and touched the tassel on His robe, for she said to herself, 'If I can just touch His robe, I'll be made well!'" (Matt. 9:20–21 HCSB).

I can identify with that distressed and needy woman. I can understand how she must have felt when she thought, *If only I can stretch out my hand and touch him, he will heal me. If only I can put one finger on his garment, he will restore my life.* She might have hesitated for a moment, wondering, *Who am I, to reach out to the Son of God? He's too important to stop and bother with me. Look at all these other people who need him, who are calling out his name and pleading for his attention.* But she knew that in a heartbeat he would pass by. He would be on his way to some other village, some other town, and her last chance for help would be gone.

In that moment, hope and faith overcame fear, and she reached out to Jesus. It's possible that when Jesus felt her gentle tug and spun around, the woman was startled and shrank back, suddenly afraid that he was going to chide her, and that her desperate gesture would bring on a rebuke.

There was no chance of that. "But Jesus turned and saw her. 'Have courage, daughter,' He said. 'Your faith has made you well.' And the woman was made well from that moment" (Matt. 9:22 HCSB).

I want to be that woman, made whole and well again by faith. Life may try to shatter us, but as author and pastor Frederick Buechner has said, we are meant to be complete in God.[2] Faith calls us to put the pieces back together and live with joy.

As God's children, we have the right to claim an inheritance of hope through Jesus. It's our privilege to be released from worry as we stay in the Word and in prayer. It's our blessing to find deep healing as faith illuminates the road before us.

May your life blossom under the Master's hand. Friends— believe the Good News!

Seeds of Faith

God, when I stand at the crossroads, make the way clear to me. Be my constant companion as I walk in faith. Thank you for loving me! Amen.

The LORD your God is with you,
he is mighty to save.
He will take great delight in you,
he will quiet you with his love,
he will rejoice over you with singing.
Zephaniah 3:17 NIV

Notes

Chapter 1

1. Marc Labonte and Linda Levine, "The 'Jobless Recovery' from the 2001 Recession: A Comparison to Earlier Recoveries and Possible Explanations," The Library of Congress, 12 August 2004, http://digitalcommons.ilr.cornell.edu/key_workplace/192.

2. Beth Moore, *Believing God* (Nashville: Broadman & Holman Publishers, 2004), 222–29.

Chapter 2

1. Fil Anderson, *Running on Empty: Contemplative Spirituality for Overachievers* (Colorado Springs, CO: Waterbrook Press, 2004), 7.

2. Ibid., 12.

3. Ibid., 15.

4. Anne Lamott, *Traveling Mercies: Some Thoughts on Faith* (New York: Pantheon Books, 1999), 40–44.

Chapter 3

1. Kay Arthur, *As Silver Refined: Learning to Embrace Life's Disappointments* (Colorado Springs, CO: Waterbrook Press, 1997), 45–46.

Chapter 4

1. Richard Foster, "Deepening Our Conversation with God, Part Two," ChristianityToday.com, from an interview with Henri Nouwen, from *Christianity Today International/ Leadership Journal* (Winter 1997) XVIII, no. 1: 112. http://www.christianitytoday.com/biblestudies/areas/biblestudies/articles/060628.html.

2. J. Brent Bill, *Holy Silence: The Gift of Quaker Spirituality* (Brewster, MA: Paraclete Press, 2005), 52–54.

3. John Ball, "The Corporate Monk," unpublished essay (April 2006).

Chapter 5

1. Janet Holm McHenry, *PrayerWalk: Becoming a Woman of Prayer, Strength, and Discipline* (Colorado Springs, CO: Waterbrook Press, 2001).

Chapter 6

1. Reynolds Price, *A Whole New Life: An Illness and a Healing* (New York: Scribner Classics, 2000), 179.

Chapter 7

1. Rick Warren, *The Purpose-Driven Life: What on Earth Am I Here For?* (Grand Rapids, MI: Zondervan, 2002), 213.

Chapter 8

1. Amy Blackmarr, *Going to Ground: Simple Life on a Georgia Pond* (New York: Viking, 1997), xi–xii, 102–103.

2. Annie Dillard, *Pilgrim at Tinker Creek* (New York: Harper Perennial, 1974), 11–13.

3. Sue Monk Kidd, *When the Heart Waits: Spiritual Direction for Life's Sacred Questions* (San Francisco: HarperSan Francisco, 1992), 5, 77.

Chapter 10

1. Barbara Kantrowitz and Pat Wingert, "The Ten Best Schools in the World," *Newsweek* (2 December 1991).

2. Ann Doss Helms, "Reggio Emilia: A New Way of Seeing Children," *Seattle Times* (5 August 1997).

3. Daniel Goleman, Paul Kaufman, and Michael Ray, *The Creative Spirit* (Plume Books, 1993), 81–85.

4. Warren, *The Purpose-Driven Life,* 173.

Chapter 12

1. Sam Dillon, "A Great Year for Ivy League Schools, but Not So Good for Applicants to Them," *New York Times* (4 April 2007); www.nytimes.com/2007/04/04/education/04colleges.html?scp=2&sq=&st+nyt.

Chapter 13

1. Lynn Coulter, "A Good Yarn: Why People and Others Flock to Brenda McKaig," Delta *Sky* (July 2004), 76–79.

Chapter 14

1. Anna B. Warner, verse 1 of "Jesus Loves Me," 1860, in the public domain; verses 2 and 3 written by David R. McGuire, in the public domain.

2. Frederick Buechner, "Journey Toward Wholeness," *Theology Today* 49, no. 4 (January 1993): 454–64.